OPTIONS TRADING

DISCOVER THE MOST INTELLIGENT STRATEGIES TO MAXIMIZE PROFIT AND LEARN TO MAKE MONEY EASILY

RICHARD GLEN

COPYRIGHT

CONTENTS

INTRODUCTION

An option is basically an agreement on the underlying shares of stock. It's an agreement to exchange shares at a fixed price over a certain timeframe (they can be bought or sold). The first thing that you should understand about options is the following. Why would someone get involved with the options trading in the first place? Most people come to options trading with the hope of earning profits from trading the options themselves. And that's probably going to describe most readers of this book. But to truly understand what you're doing, you need to understand why options exist, to begin with.

There are probably three main reasons that options on stocks exist. The first reason is that it allows people that have shares of stock to earn money from their investment in the form of regular income. So, it can be an alternative to dividend income or even enhance dividend income. If you own a minimum of 100 shares of some stock, this is a possibility. Then you can sell options against the stock and earn income from that over time intervals lasting from a week to a month, generally speaking. Obviously, such a move entails some risk, but people will enter positions of that type when the relative risk is low.

The second reason that people get involved with options is that they offer insurance against a collapse of the stock. So, once again, an option involves being able to trade shares of the stock at a fixed price that is set at the time the contract is originated. One type of contract allows the buyer to purchase shares, the other allows the buyer to sell shares. This allows people who own large numbers of shares to purchase something that provides protection of their investment that would allow them to sell the shares at a fixed price, in the event that their stock was declining by huge amounts on the market. So, the concept is exactly like paying insurance premiums. It's unclear how many people actually use this in practice, but this is one of the reasons that options exist. The way this would work would be that you pay someone a premium to secure the right to sell them your stock at a fixed price over some time frame. Then if the share price drops well below that degree to price, you would still be able to sell your shares and avoid huge losses that were occurring on the market.

The third reason that I would give for the existence of options is that it provides a way for people to make arrangements to purchase shares of stock at the prices that they find attractive, which aren't necessarily available on the market. So, there is a degree of speculation here. But let's just say that a particular stock you are interested in is trading at $100 a share. Furthermore, let's assume that people are extremely bullish on the stock and they are expecting it to rise by a great deal in the coming weeks. Maybe, it's earnings season.

During earnings season, stock can move by huge amounts. But before the earnings call, nobody knows whether the stock is going to go up or down or by how much it's going to move. An options contract could allow someone to speculate and set up a situation where they could profit from a huge move upward without having to actually invest in the stock.

So in that situation, if the stock declined instead, they wouldn't be out of much money. Just for an example, let's say they buy an options contract that allows them to purchase the shares (of the stock currently at $100) for $102, and the option costs two dollars per share. So, the stock would have to go to $104 or higher to make it worth it.

Typically, options contracts involve 100 shares. So, if the speculator bets wrong, the most they would be out would be $200.

Let's just say, after the earnings call, the share price jumps to $120. The speculator can exercise the option, which means they buy the shares at $102 per share. Then they can sell the stock on the market at the price of $120 per share. Taking into account the investment to buy the options contract, that basically leaves them with the sixteen $16 dollars per-share profit. Now, you might say well why didn't they just buy the shares that $100 a share? The reason is if they did that, they would actually be exposed to the stock to the fullest extent possible. Like we said, earnings calls can go both ways. Just recently, Netflix announced that they lost subscribers. In after-hours trading alone, the stock lost $43 per share. So, in our little example, we could say that the stock dropped instead of gaining, let's say to $80 per share. In that case, our speculator would've been in a major point of pain had they actually purchase the shares ahead of time. By doing the option instead, they set themselves up for profit while only risking a $200 loss. And it turns out that there are strategies you can use with options to profit no matter which way the stock moves. So, I didn't want to get too far ahead of ourselves, but an experienced options trader would have set up a trade designed to earn profits either way.

Types of Options

Options agreements come in two varieties. The first type of options contract is known as a call. A call option gives the buyer the possibility to buy some shares of stock at a fixed price. Usually, it's 100 shares. The agreed-upon value used to trade the shares is called the strike price. Every option comes with an expiration date, and so, if the buyer decides to purchase the shares, they must do so before the option expires. If the buyer decides to buy the shares, they are said to "exercise" the option. The party that sold to open the option, in that case, is said to be "assigned" if someone exercises the contract.

Options can be classified by the way they can be exercised. The possibilities are American-style or European-style. If you can exercise the option on any date, it's known as American style.

If the contract is a European style, the option can only be exercised on the day it expires. It's important to note that these terms don't necessarily mean that the option is trading in Europe or America. Although most options in America are American-style, there are some that are European style. Two examples are SPX and RUT. These are options used to follow the S & P 500 index and the Russell 2000 index. But the vast majority of options you're going to come across are going to be American style. If you sell options, this is something you need to be aware of. That means at any time that the option is an open position for you as a seller, you could be assigned.

The basic rule for a call option is that this is a bullish purchase. If you invest in a call option, your expectation is that's the price of the shares is going to rise. There are two ways that you can take advantage of this. The first way is to simply trade the option. Small moves in the stock price translate into big moves for options prices. So, if the stock goes up in price, you can sell the option and make a profit.

The second way to profit would be to actually exercise the right to buy the shares. In that situation, you would buy the shares for the price per share given by the strike and then sell them on the open market to make a profit. In order to make money, the price on the market must rise to a level greater than the strike price added to the amount you paid to buy in the position.

So, if you purchased a $50 option for $1, meaning the strike price is $50, the price on the market would have to rise to $51 or higher to make exercising the option profitable.

The rule is that call options increase in price or value primarily when stock prices are rising. But, as we'll see, options are impacted by some other factors as well. But the general bet with a call option is earning profits when the underlying stock goes up in value.

Before we move on to consider the other major class of options, we need to make a clear distinction between selling and buying options.

We can loosely use this language, but, actually, be applying it in very different contexts. First, let's consider simple options trading which is what most readers are going to be interested in. In this case, you enter a position by purchasing an option. So in market jargon, we would say that you are buying to open. So, in other words, you open your position by purchasing an option. If you buy to open an option you are never at risk of being assigned the shares of stock. So, you can sell the option and that carries no risk to you whatsoever. The only risk that you would face would be having to sell the option for a discount compared to what you paid to enter the position.

In contrast, you can also sell to open an options position. When you do that, you are at risk for the assignment with regard to the shares of stock. So that doesn't entail some risk but there are many reasons that people would choose to sell to open an options position. We will be exploring those later because selling to open a position can be an important part of options strategies. Also, you can sell to open positions in order to earn income from the premium.

The second type of option is called a put. A put option is a contract that allows the buyer to sell shares to the writer of the contract. This would be 100 of stock with a price given by the strike price. So, a put option has a strike price and expiration date just like a call option.

Put options actually increase in value if the market price of the stock declines. So if you buy a put, you are basically shorting the stock. If you intend to exercise the option, it would work in the following way. To use specific numbers, consider an example with the strike price of the option at $100 dollars per share. Then we will suppose that the company had a negative earnings call and the share price drop to $70 a share overnight. If you held the put option, you could buy the shares on the market at $70 a share. Then you can "exercise the option". That means you would sell the shares at the price of $100 a share because that was the strike price on the contract. So, you would make nearly a

$30 profit per share by engaging in this trade. The profit would be given by the strike price minus the premium paid to buy the option minus the price you purchase the shares for on the market. So if we just imagine that the option cost $2 a share, the profit, in this case, would be $100 - $2 - $70 = $28 per share. Since there are 100 shares per option contract, that would mean a profit of $2800.

The general rule for put options, as we said, is that they increase in value when the share price drops. So many options traders are not looking to actually exercise the option. What they want to do is still hold the put option if there is a belief that the share price will decline, and then trade the put option on the market at a profit if the share price actually drops.

So, you might ask why would someone sell to open a put option? People sell put options in order to make money from the premiums. This can be done alone or in conjunction with a special option strategy that may involve both types of options. If you sell a put option, obviously you're hoping that the share price is not going to drop far enough to make it worth it to exercise. And in most circumstances, that's actually going to be the case. A higher risk here would be selling to open a put with a strike price that is near current market prices.

Some Industry Jargon

Okay, so let's get some jargon out of the way so that you can navigate the options markets and understand what people are talking about.

Strike Price

If an option is actually exercised, shares are traded at the strike price. So, this is the price per share that the shares of stock would be sold to a buyer if we are talking about a call option. If instead, it's a put option, this is the price per share that the trader who sold to open the contract agrees to pay in order to purchase the shares from the buyer of an option. The strike price is set when the contract is opened and is good until the option expires.

Expiration Date

Every option comes with an expiration date. When trading options, it's important to know when the expiration date is. If you are only trading options with no intent to exercise them, you don't want to ever be stuck with an option on the expiration day. Options typically expire on Fridays, but for heavily traded options on exchange-traded funds, they expire Monday, Wednesday, and Friday. A "standard" option is one that lasts a month. These options will expire on a Friday. It will be the third week of the month, but there are options that only last for one week (called "weeklies") and there are also options that last several weeks to two years. An option that lasts for more than a year is called "LEAPS" which means Long-term Equity Appreciation Security. There is nothing special about them other than the expiration date, otherwise, they are just like other options.

Time Decay

Since something that expires has less value the less time there is available on the contract, options suffer from a problem called "time decay". Options get some of the pricing from "extrinsic" or "time" value. The smaller the amount of time remaining on the contract, the lower the time value. If the stock is moving in a favorable direction, however, the value of the option that is related to the current market cost of the stock and a couple of other factors can overwhelm time decay.

To know what the time decay is, you can look up a quantity called theta that will be listed for every option. It will tell you how much the option price is going to drop at the market open the following day. So, if an option has a theta of -0.11, that means that it's going to drop in price by 100 shares x $0.11 = $11 at the next market open. This may or may not be important. Other factors can swamp that $11 and make it irrelevant. But you need to be aware of it.

In-the-Money

If the strike price favorably positioned with respect to current market prices, it is known by this term. For a call option, it will be in the money if the share price (on the market) of the stock is greater than the price known as the strike price. For a put option, it will be in the money if the price that would be paid for the stock just buying it is less than the strike price.

When an option is in the money, its value has heavily influenced the price that the stock is trading at. In the ideal situation, which can happen as an in the money call option approaches expiration, a $1 increase in the stock price will translate into a $100 change in the price of the option that would go up as well. Of course, this cuts both ways, so it can mean a $100 loss if the share price is moving the other way.

At the Money

If the strike price is exactly the same as the share price on the market, it is known by this phrase. At the money, options can offer a relatively low priced way to enter a trade and take advantage of the movements in share price that are likely to make it go in the money if you have done your homework and entered a good trade.

Out of the Money

For a call option, it's said to be in this state if the strike price is greater than the market price. If the option expires out of the money, it is said to expire worthlessly. For a put option, it will be out of the money if the share price is above the strike price.

CHAPTER 1: THE RIGHT MENTALITY TO START A TRADER'S PATH

There are many skills and abilities that traders possess and that they need to experience market success when trading. They have to understand how the company works, and they must be able to determine the general direction of the trend of a stock. These are just but technical skills that are needed to survive in the sometimes- harsh terrain that is trading. Many times, the soft skills associated with the trade are ignored, and yet they are as important to the trader's success as much as the technical skills are. Some of these include:

• Ability to remain calm and contain emotion

• Ability to think quickly

• Discipline

These skills may look ordinary, but they hold deep importance for traders, and that is why they are commonly referred to as trading psychology. Trading psychology is important because to trade successfully; traders need aspects of it to think fast, make equally fast decisions and dart in and out of stocks on a short leash. They need a presence of mind to accomplish these goals. When a trader has a trading plan, they need to use trading psychology to stick to their goals. They also need trading psychology to know when to book losses and profits without letting emotions get in their way.

Some of the emotions experienced by traders include:

Fear. Traders feel fearful when they receive negative news related to the market in general or about a certain stock. Mostly, their direct reaction is an overreaction in which they feel forced to liquidate their holdings and refrain from taking any further risks.

They feel that by taking these actions, they are avoiding losses. However, most time, as a trader, you will realize that while avoiding loss, you will also miss out on bargains. Sometimes, just after you have liquidated, you may find that the scales start tilting in your favor, and that is how you miss out on something with great potential. Traders tend to experience fear during bear markets and can have devastating effects when it goes a notch higher and turns into a panic, causing investors to make selloffs as a result of panic selling.

Thankfully, fear is a natural reaction that we have as humans. We react this way to what we feel are threats. In this case, you feel that your money-making and profit-making potential is under threat. However, this does not mean that you should let the mention override your objectives in the market; you should find ways to go around it. For example, you can quantify the fear by considering how much fear you experience and what scares you the most. By having these thoughts well in advance of the occurrences, there is a likelihood that you will be mentally prepared for any eventuality and should a situation that scares you come by, you may know how to react non-instinctively in your favor. When you think about unpleasant situations, it gives you the ability to isolate yourself when they happen during the trade session and identify them. This is not something that you will understand how to do right off the bat. Normally, you will have to learn it over time, like an art. You will have to work on your skills over time so that you can be sure that you will be keeping your portfolio healthy instead of making decisions that can cause ill financial health in the end.

Greed. It is not uncommon to hear the saying "pigs get eaten" on Wall Street. Wall Street is the holy ground of traders and where the biggest players on the stock exchange play. Hearing such simple yet profound words from such a highly regarded place should tell you something. In reality, they do not mean literal pigs get slaughtered. Instead, they refer to greedy investors, like pigs.

Usually, when you win, you may get the urge to hang onto positions you feel are winning, hoping to get every last tick. This can be tricky because you run a much bigger risk of being blown out of a position or getting whipsawed.

Greed is a big temptation, especially when things are going your way, so it has to take a great amount of will-power to overcome it. Just like fear, greed is a natural instinct that pushes you as a trader towards doing better by giving just a little more. As such, investors may take actions such as making high-risk trades hoping for profits, buying shares of an untested technology because of an upward price trend, or buying shares prior to doing their groundwork. You can also find yourself staying in a trade for longer than is advisable simply because you feel that you may squeeze out a few extra bucks from it and thus, this emotion is most prominent in the final phase of bull markets where investors usually like to take their guard down. You should learn to recognize when your greed button is almost getting turned on and switch it off effectively. Much like every other emotion, you will encounter on this list; you will need to exercise patience when trying to deal with greed. You will learn over time how and when it is best to best count your profits and take leave.

Hope and regret. Hope and regret are like two sides of a coin. While fear and greed are the primary drivers of most traders, fear and regret take a close position behind them because they also influence the decisions of investors in a significant amount of cases. For instance, when a trader feels fearful, and they liquidate their holdings, they may feel that they are missing out when things start looking up again. A trader may also regret and get into a trade after missing out initially as a result of stock moving too fast, sadly, this is a violation of trading discipline, something that all traders strive for and the results are always not favorable as they result in direct losses when security prices begin to fall from those peak highs. Hope and regret may work hand in hand because after regretting missing out, traders get back into the market with the hope of gaining on what they missed.

How to build a successful trading mentality and eliminate poor habits

Building a successful trading mentality does not come easy. However, it is not impossible. There are habits that you can eliminate from your routine and those you can add to successfully adjust and become a psychologically fit trader.

Check your posture. Before starting to trade and throughout the day, ensure that you take a moment to consider your physical posture if you find yourself slouching with your neck bending forward or backward, correct the sitting position by sitting up upright and straightening your spine. Your posture affects how you breathe and how you think. When you slouch, energy does not flow smoothly through your body from up to down, and it impairs blood flow from the head to heart. You, therefore, do not think clearly. Also, when your head bends either backward or forwards, it cuts down energy flow to the spine, which can make you stuck in your head, literally. Keeping your head up and rectifying your posture can help you have a clear head that will enable you to trade better.

Find ways to increase your focus. As you read this book, find ways to increase your focus and concentration. You could take simple steps such as turning off the television, turning off the internet browser, turning off your cell phone, stopping email checks or you could take advanced actions such as meditating before you start your day. Meditating improves concentration and thus, can be beneficial for your trading. Then after meditation, you should focus on the markets that you want to trade for the day. Once you have tried this habit for a few days, check how your focus was impacted, and if it has changed your trading experience in any way. If you like the results of the new habit, you can as well make it a permanent part of your routine.

Check your energy levels as you trade throughout the day. If you are not using the end-of-day trading routine, this tip can work well for you. Before you sit down to trade and at several points during the day, you should ask yourself if your overall energy level is high when you start trading or if it is low. It may help to place it on a scale of 1 to 10 with 10 expressing optimal energy and 1 expressing minimal energy. If your energy is weak, figure out whether it is physical or mental. If it is physical, check on things such as posture, whether you have eaten and drank enough water and feel your body generally to get an idea of what is going on. If it is mental, then it would be a good time to task yourself by tapping into your mind to find out if you are engaging in any negative thought patterns, and once you become aware of what is happening, you should take a moment to clear your head, for example, through meditation, before resuming work.

This strategy is a powerful one and can be done at several key points in your day, or you could schedule it as part of your trade routine. If your energy levels fall below your standards of what should be ideal and you are having a difficult time rectifying it, it is better to take some time off before resuming trade as these low energy levels may interfere with your ability to make the right decisions. If you feel that your body is just fine, on the other hand, then do not waste this opportunity on anything else. Use it to trade as there is a likelihood that you will make the best decisions in this way.

Inculcate positive thoughts. Now that you understand the kind of bearing negative thoughts may have on your success as a trader, you must find a remedy. While it may go contrary to your feelings and emotions, deliberately choosing positive actions will help build your confidence and experience. Positive thoughts do more than we can imagine. Your vision becomes more panoramic, you become a stable trader, your determination is enhanced, and you have a renewed, deep understanding of the market. Over time, you will be able to trade confidently over days, months, and years. You will no longer have excuses for what you have not done, cut down on procrastination, and not subscribe to your emotions, which are dangerous for a trader.

Take the trading market as a platform on which you can challenge yourself and prove through your actions that your positive attitude is paying off. Choose a time every day where you will say positive affirmations to yourself as this will be a crucial step in determining how your day. Talk to yourself confidently, getting yourself out of mental laziness, emotionality, and hesitation. This self-talk is important as your subconscious mind rewires itself to help you achieve the positive goals you have. This can be one of the first steps you take towards financial wealth and stability. If you make this a part of your routine for a week or two, you can take time to check your progress. If you like the results, you can choose to make this a part of your routine.

The 5% rule. Resolve that for the next trading week; you will give just 5% more of your energy to trading. To make use of this rule, identify the areas where you perceive yourself to be poor, and need development. The extra 5% of your time should be dedicated to strengthening your weaknesses in these areas. Over a few weeks, you will notice that this method has yielded results as there will be a difference in your trading, mindset, or the results of your trading. You can then decide to take it a notch higher by putting in an extra 10% of your time, or you can decide to make the 5% final and part of your routine.

The tips and tactics above will help you develop positive trade ethics. The secret to knowing what works for you is through evaluating results. That is why, at every step, I ensured that I asked that you check how you trade after a few days or weeks of the tactics. Note how your trade experience changes and see what you have accomplished and if you can use the experience to continue developing your forex trading skills. When this happens, you will have a self-reinforcing process that eliminates the need for a mentor. In short, you will become a self-taught master trader.

To control your emotions, two main strategies can help you:

Setting rules well in advance. As a trader, you should learn to get your head in the right place before you get psychological crunches. As such, it would be wise to lay out guidelines for any trade based on your risk tolerance and have a plan for when you will enter and exit the trade. You will need to know whether a stop loss or profit target will be the exit signal and take all emotion out of the trading process. You can also decide that in the wake of some events such as macroeconomic news and positive or negative earnings.

You can also consider setting limits to the amount of money you are willing to lose or win in a day. If you hit your profit target, take your earnings, and stop for the day. If the loss hits the limit, it is also time to pack up and go as leaving will prevent you from further losses

Doing research and assessments. As a trader, it is upon you to learn as much as you can about your area of interest. Educate yourself through reading and go for seminars and conferences that relate to your interests. As directed above, ensure that you dedicate a certain amount of time to research. Take part in activities that help build your knowledge base, such as studying charts, reading trade journals, and studying the analysis methods of the trade so that you are up to speed even before you start trading. Remember to remain flexible and consider experimenting with different techniques and instruments time and again. For instance, you can set stop losses at different places. To ensure that you are learning well, do your experiments within reason.

CHAPTER 2: DIFFERENCES AMONG FOREX, STOCKS AND OPTIONS TRADING

There are different reasons some traders love to use forex instead of the stock market. One of them is the forex leverage. We will look at the disparities that exist between forex trading and stock trading.

1.Leverage

When it comes to stock trading, you tend to trade with a cap of leverage of two to one. You must have some requirements on the ground before these can be done. It is not every investor than ends up being approved for that margin account, and this is what a trader needs to be leveraged in a typical stock market.

When it comes to forex trading, the entire system is totally different. Before you can trade using leverage, you need to have opened the forex trading account. That's the only requirement that is out there, nothing else. When you open a forex account, you can easily use the leverage feature.

If you are trading in the United States of America, you will be restricted to a leveraging of 50:1 leveraging. Countries outside of the US are restricted to leverage of about 200:1. It is better when you are outside the US, than in the US.

2.Liquidity differences

When you decide to trade stocks, you end up purchasing the companies' shares that have a cost from a bit of dollars down to even hundreds of dollars. Usually, the price in the market tends to share with demand and supply.

Paired trades

When you trade with forex, you are facing another world, unseen in the stock market. Though the currency of a country tends to change, there will always be a great supply of currency that you can trade. What this means is that the main currencies in the world tend to be very liquid.

When you are in forex trading, you will see that the currencies are normally quoted in pairs. They are not quoted alone. This means that you should be interested in the country's economic health that you have decided to trade in. The economic health of the country tends to affect the worth of the currency.

The basic considerations change from one forex market to the next. If you decide to purchase the Intel shares, the main aim is to see if the stock's value will improve. You aren't interested in how the prices of other stocks are.

On the other hand, if you have decided to sell or buy forex, you need to analyze the economies of those countries that are involved in the pairs.

You should find out if the country has better jobs, GDP, as well as political prospects.

To do a successful trade in the Forex market, you will be expected to analyze not only one financial entity, but two.

The forex market tends to show higher level of sensitivity in upcoming economic and political scenarios in many countries.

You should note that the U.S. stock market, unlike many other stock markets is not so sensitive to a lot of foreign matters.

3.Price sensitivity to trade activities

When we look at both markets, we have no choice but to notice that there is varying price sensitivity when it comes to trade activities done.

If a small company that has fewer shares has about ten thousand shares bought from it, it could go a long way to impact the price of the stock. For a big company such as Apple, such n number of shares when bought from it won't affect the stock price.

When you look at forex trades, you will realize that trades of a few hundreds of millions of dollars won't affect the major currency at all. If it affects, it would be minute.

4.Market accessibility

It is easy to access the currency market, unlike its counterpart, the stock market. Though you may be able to trade stocks every second of the day, five days weekly in the twenty first century, it is not easy.

A lot of retail investors end up trading via a United States brokerage that makes use of a single major trading period every day, which spans from 9:30 AM to 4:00 PM. They go ahead to have a minute trading hour past that time, and this period has price and volatility issues, which end up dissuading a lot of retail traders from making use of such time.

Forex trading is different. One can carry out such trading every second of the day because there are a lot of forex exchanges in the world, and they are constantly trading in one time zone or the other.

Forex Trading Vs Options

A trader may believe the United States Dollar will become better when compared to the Euro, and if the results pan out, the person earns.

The strategy, if it works, can help in affecting the trade when the research pans out.

When you get involved in Options Trading, you tend to get involved in the purchase and sales of options on great amounts of futures, stocks and so on, that will move either up or below at a price during the phase.

It is similar to Forex Trading, since you can easily leverage the buying power to have a controlling power on futures or stocks.

There exist a number of disparities that exist between Options trading and Forex trading. They are:

1. 24 Hour Trading:

When you get involved in Forex instead of Options trading, you have the capability of trading every second of the day, five days weekly. When you look at the Forex market, you will realize that it lives longer than any financial market in the world.

If you have decided to get double digit gains in the market, it is important to possess a generous amount of time every week to carry out these trades. If a large event occurs anywhere in the world, you may end up being amongst the first to benefit from the situation in the Foreign Exchange market.

You don't expect to spend time waiting and hoping that the market opens in the market like in the case of trading options.

With Forex, you can easily trade anytime you want, at all times of the night and day. Whenever you wish, you can trade it.

2.Rapid Trade Execution:

When you immediately make use of the Forex market; you tend to get instantaneous trade executions. You don't have to be delayed like in the case of Options or some other markets too.

When you place the order, it ends up being filled using the best potential price in the market, instead of wondering what price ends up being ordered.

You won't have to have the urge to slip like the case of options. When you are involved in Foreign Exchange Trading, there is a great chance of liquidity unlike in the case of Options trading.

3.No Commissions:

Forex market is one that doesn't need commission because it acts as an inter-bank market, where buyers are matched with sellers instantly.

There aren't cases of brokerage fees like in the stock market and other markets.

You will see a spread that exists between ask price and the bid, that is the way a lot of Forex trading firms earn their money.

What this means is that when you trade Forex, you stand to save the brokerage fees unlike in the case of options trading, where you are expected to pay communion since you have no choice but to use a brokerage firm.

Forex Trading Risks

Like every financial market out there, there are risks that one may have to face. The interbank market is known to have different degrees of regulations. Apart from that, forex instruments aren't as standardized as other financial market instruments out there. Do you know that in some parts of the globe, there are no regulations to the forex market?

The interbank market consists of different banks all over the world trading with one another.

The banks have no choice but to determine an asset to credit risk and sovereign risks. They have come up with different internal processes, in a bid to ensure that they remain quite safe. These types of regulations are imposed in the industry to ensure that every participating bank is protected.

The market pricing comes from the forces of demand and supply because the market is made up of different banks giving bids and offers.

The fact that there is a great amount of trade flows in the market means that rogue investors can't influence the worth of a currency. This ensures that there is transparency in the foreign exchange market for those traders that are privy to interbank dealing.

A lot of countries have regulations concerning the forex, but not all do. Pros and Cons of Forex

First Pro:

When it comes to a daily trading volume in every market out there, the forex is the largest, meaning that it possesses the largest amount of liquidity.

This is one reason that one can easily enter or exit a position whenever he wants, for a small spread in a lot of market conditions.

Cons:

Brokers, banks and dealers are known to give a great level of leverage, meaning that investors can easily control huge positions using a tiny amount of money.

Though you don't see it every time, a high ratio of leverage of 100:1 is possible to see in the foreign exchange market. It is important that a trader knows how to use leverage, as well as the risks that using leverage brings to an account. Using a large amount of leverage has forced a lot of dealers to become bankrupt unexpectedly.

Second Pro

You can trade in the foreign exchange market every second of the day, six days in a week. It usually begins daily in Australia and ends in New York.

The main centers for forex are Singapore, Hong Kong, Sydney, Tokyo, New York, London and Paris.

Second Con

Before you can trade currencies in a profitable manner, you have to understand economic indicators and basics. A currency investor has to possess a great understanding of how a lot of economies function, as well as how connected they are. You need to understand these fundamentals that are able to alter the values of currencies.

What Is A Stock

Stock is sometimes called equity or shares. This is a kind of security that shows proportionate ownership when the firm that issues it is concerned. When a person has stocks, he/she is entitled to a proportion of the earnings and assets of the company.

One can buy stocks and sell them on stock exchanges, but this doesn't mean that there aren't other ways of buying and selling stocks. Stocks can also be exchanged in private sales. There is hardly any investor in the financial world that doesn't have stocks in their portfolio.

Before the transactions can be said to be legitimate, they must be in line with the government regulations that have been put in place to shield investors from fraudulent processes.

When compared to a lot of financial instruments, stocks have overshadowed them.

Stock Vs Bond

Companies give out stocks to raise the needed capital to improve their business or get involved in new projects.

Shares can be gotten in different ways. Sometimes, a person may purchase it directly from the firm when it issues it in the primary market. In other cases, the investor may purchase it in the secondary market from another shareholder. Whenever you see a corporation issuing shares, know that it carries it out because it wants to raise money.

Bonds are in another world of its own. Bondholders are seen as creditors to the firm, and they tend to get interest instead of dividends. They are also paid the principal.

When it comes to stakeholders in a company, creditors have more right over the assets and earnings than shareholders when bankruptcy occurs.

The corporation is expected to pay shareholders first before it pays shareholders during a bankruptcy. Shareholders end up being the last in line and may end up getting nothing or a little amount. What this means is that stocks have higher risks than bonds.

If you can't stomach this, you should avoid going for stocks. What are The Options

Options are those contracts that allow the bearer to be involved in the purchase or sales of a stipulated amount of asset at a fixed price. The bearer has the choice to buy or not, as long as the contract hasn't expired.

Options are bought like a lot of asset classes by making use of brokerage investment accounts.

Options are strong to the extent that they can improve the portfolio of an individual. They can get this done by leverage and added income protection.

Based on the scenarios at hand, different option situations can suit the goals of an investor.

Let's say a stock market is declining; options can be used as an effective hedge to clamp down on downside losses. One can use options to get recurring income. They can also be utilized for speculative purposes like wagering on where the stock price would go.

The way that free lunch doesn't exist in bonds and stocks is the same way that there is no free lunch with options.

There are some risks that one may face when options trading is concerned. You have to understand these risks before you jump into options trading.

This is one reason that when you have decided to trade options with a brokerage company, you are shown a disclaimer that is similar to this:

Options are members of a bigger league of securities, which are called derivatives. The price of a derivative is linked to the price of another thing. Let's make things more transparent. The derivative of a tomato is ketchup. The derivative of grapes is wine. The derivative of a stock is a stock option.

Options can be said to be derivatives of financial securities, meaning that their worth is dependent on another asset's price.

Some examples of derivatives are puts, calls, forwards, futures, and so on.

Call and Put Options

When we say that options are derivative securities, we mean that their rice is related to the pricing of another thing. This means that the other thing is what controls the price of the options.

If you purchase the options contract, you are given the right to buy or sell an asset at a stimulate price before the deal expires. You aren't under compulsion to do this.

When a person has a call option, he is given the right to purchase a stock. On the other hand, when a person is given a put option, he has the right to sell the stock.

You can see the call option as a form of down-payment for something that can be gotten in the future.

Let's use a more explicit example. A person sees a new building going up. He may want to have the right to buy it later but says he won't buy it until it has gotten to some stage, or some other condition has been

met, this is an example of an option. He can decide to use the option or not. He isn't under compulsion.

Let's say the developer agrees to give the person the right to purchase the house for about a million dollars at any time within the next three years. Before the developer can agree with this, the prospective buyer has to pay a down payment, which can't be refundable. Within that period of three years, the developer isn't allowed to sell the house to anyone else, until after the term expires.

CHAPTER 3: WE ANALYZE THE MARKET

Options traders understand that they can make money in any market environment, even when the prevailing market is not trading up or down. This is possible due to the versatility and flexibility of options contracts; however, some of the approaches used to make money in any market environment are as complex and risky as they are flexible. Fortunately, options traders can tailor their trading strategies to be aggressive, conservative, or somewhere in between when facing any particular market condition.

Whether an individual is an investor or a trader, his or her main goal is to make a profit. The secondary objective is to make money with a minimum level of risk acceptable. In options trading, prices do not always behave as people expect. This unpredictability could cause traders to incur unexpected losses or leave money on the table.

The modern market environment offers tons of opportunities for options traders. However, some risks come with these opportunities. Essentially, the higher the level of volatility in the market, the greater the risk is. Experienced traders and investors are attracted to the options market as a way to make money from price changes while limiting their risk to a certain dollar amount.

However, they have to do it right. For example, builders who only use a hammer, even if they are skilled at using it, cannot build a house. They need to be able to use a drill, saw, level, square, and other tools needed to do the job properly. In the same way, options traders need to be able to use different strategies to build the trading accounts and profits they desire.

They should be constantly aware of how their trades are sensitive to implied volatility, time, and changes in price and adjust their positions according to the market environment. Although options traders are not market makers, they can still benefit themselves by learning how different factors affect the value of different options.

Trends and Ranges

The choice of trading trends or ranges is one of the most important choices when it comes to options trading. In order to make a smart choice, traders need to assess the price movements to enhance their chances of success greatly. Ranges and trends are two distinct price properties requiring somewhat opposing money-management techniques and mindsets. Fortunately, the options market is uniquely suited to accommodate both approaches while offering opportunities for making money.

We can define a trend as a lower high in a downtrend and a higher low in an uptrend. Many options traders spend a significant portion of their time hunting for trends in the stock charts in the hope of riding the next trend to profit. Unfortunately, they forget to look at sideways price action, which can be just as profitable. When a stock stops following a trend and swings up and down between two prices instead, it becomes range-bound.

Range-bound options establish nearly identical lows and highs, thereby creating a lower support level and a higher resistance level. This phenomenon may be frustrating for traders looking to ride a trend. However, the relative predictability of these upper and lower levels can mean easy money for a smart trader, albeit in smaller quantities.

Trend Trading

This is when options traders make trading plays based on stock price trends over a certain timeframe. Essentially, it is a systematic approach to trading based on a stock or assets' current momentum. Traders use technical tools and price movements to identify trading signals. When executed properly, it can be a time-effective and cost-effective way to make money in the options market. However, an individual need to have some stock market and technical analysis skills to use this trading technique effectively.

This style of options trading involves the following:

a) Moving averages

b) Stop-loss provisions

c) Price calculations

d) Take-profit provisions

Trading platforms have a wide range of automated signals and indicators; however, everything comes down to identifying trend indicators and oscillators. That said trend indicators are great since they are the most important tool when it comes to taking advantage of markets that are moving sharply. According to many options traders, trend trading is a sure path to making a profit. Trend indicators help turn the market trend to one's advantage. Some of the most common trend indicators found on most trading platforms are:

a) Bollinger bands

b) Ichimoku cloud

c) The moving average indicator

Trend indicators all come with default interpretations. Even if a trader does not know how to use one of these indicators, a simple Google search will solve the problem. However, applying this interpretation on actual trading can be a bit challenging because trend trading strategies are so diverse. Therefore, the secret to success is to start by defining the market, followed by applying the most ideal trading strategies for that market, and, finally, to watch for any changes that might indicate the trend is about to end.

Benefits of Trend Trading

a) Ability to make a few trades while still making money.

b) It does not require a lot of time, which is ideal for busy people looking to make extra money.

c) It does not require the same daily grind that most day traders have to go through.

d) It is less risky and allows traders to focus on trends within different industries and stocks.

Disadvantages

a) It is not for people who want to make quick money.

b) There is a potential for setting poor guidelines and restrictions because not all trends proceed as expected.

Range Trading

The truth about options trading is that markets often move sideways. It is in such market conditions that options traders do the most harm to themselves, especially when they continue to follow a trend when the market starts going sideways. However, not all range-bound market conditions are the same. A few are simply not worth trading; therefore, it is important to understand what type of range-bound markets one should choose to trade. When the market inevitably changes from a trending condition to a sideways-moving condition, an individual should do the following:

1.Determine whether the market is worth trading. If it is oscillating between certain levels of resistance and support with a good distance between the two levels, then it is worth trading.

2.If it is choppy or consolidating very tightly, then the market is not worth trading because the distance it is oscillating between will not allow for a good risk-reward ratio.

Determining the strength of resistance and support is critical to interpreting price charts when it comes to range trading. Resistance is the price level at which selling is strong enough to reverse or interrupt an upward trend in price. A near-horizontal or horizontal line connecting a number of tops on a chart represents it. Support, on the other hand, is the level where buying is strong enough to reverse or interrupt a downward trend and is supported by a horizontal line connecting a number of bottoms.

Usually, the strength of these zones depends on the trading volume, height, and length of the level. Essentially, the higher the trading volume in the zone is, the stronger the resistance and support zone. In addition, the length of the area will determine the depth of the zone.

To trade a range-bound asset successfully, a trader needs to first confirm the range. Essentially, the price of the asset needs to have reached at least two similar lows and highs without breaking below or above at any point in between. Once this range is established, he or she should simply sell puts near the resistance level and purchase calls near the support level. Experiences traders, however, may use more complicated trading strategies to play both sides of the coin at the same time.

Since the biggest potential for risk in range trading is being on the losing side of the coin, it is important to look out for any signals that might indicate when this will happen. In many situations, a range is merely a short pause or a period of indecision before the continuation of a trend. Therefore, instead of setting a stop-limit order near the resistance or support levels and simply sit back and wait, a trader should pay close attention to important price indicators.

Counter Trend

Counter-trend trending is an options trading strategy that attempts to profit from an assumption that the current trading trend will reverse. It is usually a medium-term trading strategy where an individual holds positions between several weeks or days. Traders who use this strategy rely on indicators, oscillators, and envelop channels to make their decisions. This trading strategy is useful for risk management, diversification, or pure profit.

Essentially, this strategy takes trading positions opposite to the current trend and can be applied at any time. However, traders mostly use it when they see a strong likelihood of a reversal. Usually, people call this strategy swing trading because traders aim to take advantage of swings in a new or opposite direction. Countertrend strategies are usually complex; therefore, experienced traders are the ones who mostly use them.

The idea behind this strategy is to take advantage of overpriced options in the market that is in a decline or incline. For example, if a particular stock is overpriced and has been rallying for a long period; many people assume it will continue to do so forever. Some smart options traders look for such trends and try to take advantage of the possibility of that stock being overpriced because it is in high demand. Ideally, the strategy can make money if the stock goes down, up, or sideways. However, if it continues to rise too fast too far, there is a lot of room for error.

Participation

Many options traders do not understand the participants on the other end of their trades or transactions. Trading in options is mot some mysterious process simply because it is a different form of security. In fact, it is quite similar to trading stocks. In the options market, individual traders are dealing with the following participants:

1.Retail investors just like them

2.Market makers

3.Broker-dealers

4.Institutional traders

5.Exchanges

However, all these participants are generally referred to as traders. Transactions made by each participant are routed to exchanges. Retail investors purchase and sell options using their own money to make a profit. Market makers, on the other hand, are the huge players in the game. They make offers and bids on the options on specific securities and provide liquidity in the marketplace. Essentially, they are usually ready to take a stand on the opposite side of the trade if and when the other participants in the marketplace wish to purchase or sell an option.

Broker-dealers work to make trades happen. These firms accept orders or bids on behalf of their clients and then make sure they execute them at the best price available in the open market. They do this through exchanges for a commission on each trade. In addition, dealers may also choose to sell or purchase options for their own profit, but brokers do not do this.

Institutional traders are large professional trading entities like hedge funds and mutual funds. They often trade options as pure speculation or to hedge their positions. Finally, exchanges exist to provide timely price information and to ensure an orderly and fair marketplace. They can be either an electronic platform or a physical location where traders meet to transact.

Turning Points

These are the obvious lows and highs where markets g from bearish to bullish, or vice versa. Essentially, a market turning point is the area of price reversal. Options trading market turning points stand out clearly on price charts, making them easy to identify. They can create the illusion that profitable trades are easy to catch. However, trying to do so is what causes most inexperienced options traders to suffer losses.

Tips for Trading Turning Points

1.Avoid trading initial market turning points.

2.Wait for another reversal into such a level and try to spot the fake breakout pattern or squeeze.

3.Avoid picking bottoms or tops during such a squeeze.

Options traders should think smart and avoid following the crowd trading tip that leads the majority of traders to do the same, costly mistake.

It is important to understand how to use options to accomplish one's financial objectives because these financial instruments trade differently than stocks. For the experienced options trader, this is a good thing because he or she can design strategies to profit from a wide range of market conditions with minimum risk.

CHAPTER 4: LET'S GO INTO THE DETAILS: OPTIONS TRADING TECHNICAL GRECO

Now that we know what influences the prices of options, we are going to make that more quantifiable. This is done using the so-called "Greeks," which are five parameters denoted by Greek symbols (or letters) that quantify the way the price of an option will change. You don't have to know how they work precisely, only what they mean. At any given time, you can look them up to get their values. We start by looking at intrinsic value, that is, how the price of the option changes or varies with the underlying stock's price.

Delta

If you look at the data for any option, you are going to see five Greek letters (usually expressed by their English spelled names) delta, theta, gamma, vega, and rho. The first of these is delta, which tells you how the price of an option changes with the price of the underlying stock.

We noted earlier that the price of an option doesn't have a 1-1 change in price in relation to the stock. You can see exactly how it will change by looking at delta. First, we'll consider call options. So if delta is 0.46, that means if the underlying stock price rises by $1, the price of the option is going to increase by $0.46. If delta was 0.74, then the price of the option would rise by $0.74 if the price of the underlying stock went up by $1.

Put options have a negative delta, which just indicates that a put option has an inverse relationship to the price of the underlying stock. That is if the price of the underlying stock goes down, the value of a put option goes up, and if the price of the underlying stock goes up, the value of the put option goes down.

So if delta is -0.26, and the price of the underlying stock went up by $1, the value of the put option would drop by 26 cents. On the other hand, if the price of the underlying stock had dropped by $1, then the price of the put option would rise by $0.26.

Delta is dynamic, and the number always changes when some important parameter in the options price changes. Consider an option on a stock that is trading at $102 with a strike price of $100, with 14 days to option expiration. In this case, the price of the call option is $2.48, and delta is 0.75. The price of the put option is $0.47, and delta for the put option is -0.25. So if the price of the underlying stock goes up by $1, we expect the call option to rise to $2.48 + $0.75 = $3.23. The price of the put option would decrease to $0.47 - $0.25 = $0.22.

That's just about what happens, but in reality, the relationship isn't quite exact since other things impact the price of the options. The call option increases to $3.84, and the put option declines in price to $0.27.

We said its dynamic, and what happens when the share price rises by $1, is the delta values for both options change as well. Now delta is 0.84 for the call, and -0.16 for the put.

That tells us something important, namely that delta is higher the more in the money the stock is. We can see this looking at some real options. Considering an IBM $124 call that expires on 6/28, it has a delta of 0.967. A $139 call that expires on 6/28 has a delta of 0.5388. The share price is $139.20, so the $124 call is more in the money. The $139 call is practically at the money, and we learn a second important fact about delta, that is that at the money options will have a delta that is reasonably close to 0.50.

Since the more in the money you are, the higher delta, that means in the money options can benefit (or be hurt by) a $1 change in the price of the underlying stock.

Something else that happens is that if the option is in the money, the closer you get to expiration, the higher delta goes. For our example of an option with a $100 share price, if the underlying stock price remains at $103, moving to 7 days from expiration, delta jumps to 0.92 for the call. Moving to 3 days to expiration, delta is 0.98. So if you are expecting a stock price to move a lot in the next few days, getting an option that will expire soon before the move happens could be a worthwhile investment. Look for events that could impact the price, such as an earnings call or product announcement.

Remember at the money options have a delta of about 0.50, and when you get close to expiration, delta for a call will be exactly 0.50, and for a put, it will be -0.5, if the option was at the money. Actually buying at the money options can be quite difficult, so you'll probably have to settle for something close.

If an option is out of the money, the closer to the expiration date, you get the smaller delta gets. In fact, a few days away from expiration delta can get vanishingly small. An out of the money call option for a strike price of $100, share price of $97 with three days to expiration will have a delta of 0.02.

The delta for the same put option will add up the difference to 100 (but remember it's expressed as a negative value). In this case, a put option with the same parameters, so a strike price of $100 – will have a delta of -0.98 if the underlying price is $97. In that case, the put would be worth $3.00, and if the underlying share price dropped to $96, the price of the put would rise to $4. Then you'd see delta increase to -1.00 for the put and drop to 0.00 for the call.

If the stock had moved the other way, risen in price by $1, then delta for the put would drop to -0.92 instead, and the price of the put would drop to $2.04.

The bottom line is delta will give you a good estimate of how much the price of the option will change when the price of the underlying stock changes by $1. If it's a call option, the relationship is direct, and delta is expressed as a positive number. For put options, since the relationship is an inverse one, delta is a negative number. And remember that if you take the absolute value of delta for the put option and add it to the delta value for a call option that has the same strike value and date of expiration, they will sum to 1.0.

Gamma

Gamma is like the second derivative. In other words, it tells you how delta itself changes. This is important since we noted that delta was dynamic. However, beginning traders don't need to dive into this too deeply, but you can check gamma to see about how much delta will change if there is a $1 change in the price of the underlying shares. Gamma has the same value for both puts and calls. So if Gamma were 0.22 and delta was 0.24 for a call option, and -0.76 for a put option with the same strike and expiration date, we'd expect a $1 rise in share price to cause delta for the call option to increase to 0.46, and the delta for the put option would change to -0.54. That is about what would happen, but remember if the option was at the money the values of delta would move to 0.5 and -0.5, respectively.

Theta

When examining options, theta is a very important parameter among the Greeks. What theta gives you information about is the time decay of the option. Theta is expressed as a negative number, reflecting the fact that time decay causes a decrease in option price as time goes on. Let's consider a couple of examples.

Suppose that we have call and put options with a strike price of $100 with three days to expiration. The price of the call is $1.20, and the price of the put is $0.20 if the share price of the underlying stock is

$101. In this case, theta is -0.073 for both the call and the put. That tells us that if nothing else changes, the price of each option will decrease by $0.073. The call option is priced at $1.20, and the put is priced at $0.20. Moving to 2 days to expiration and leaving everything else the same, we find that the price of the call option drops to $1.12, and the price of the put option drops to $0.12, so it moved in almost exact accordance to what was expected. The following day theta has increased to -0.079, reflecting the fact that time decay happens more rapidly the closer you get to the expiration date of the option.

In fact, with everything else unchanged, 20 days to expiration theta is about half as strong, at -0.035. That reflects one of the fundamental truths of options, that is that time decay happens in an exponential fashion, with time decay happening faster the closer you get to expiration.

One of the things that help make options seem complicated is that all of these variables are interdependent. So at 20 days to expiration, suppose the stock price shot up to $108. In that case, theta decreases to -0.005. So it's only 1/7th of the prior value. It decreases for the put option as well.

Theta is also proportional to share price. So theta is larger if the share price is larger. Consider a stock with a share price of $975, and a strike price of $1,000. In that case, theta is -0.282 for the call option and -0.274 for the put option. That means if a day passes and nothing else changes, the value of the call option (which in this case is $5.15) will drop by about $0.28, and the value of the put option will drop by about $0.27.

Check the Greek theta to get an idea of how the price of the option is going to decay by the following day if all other things are held equal.

Vega

The next Greek that we are going to meet is Vega, which tells us the relationship between the price of the option and the implied volatility. What Vega tells you is how sensitive the option is to changes in the implied volatility. Generally speaking an in the money option is less sensitive to changes in implied volatility, while an out of the money option is more sensitive to changes in implied volatility. Specifically, vega tells you how much the price of the option will change if the implied volatility changes by 1%. Remember that options that have higher implied volatility are worth more money.

Suppose a stock is trading at $500 a share, and the strike price is $490 with 10 days left to expiration and an implied volatility of 23.5%. Vega will be 0.285. A call will be priced at $13.73, and the put with the same parameters would be priced at $3.69. If the implied volatility increased to 24.5%, then the call would be priced at $14.02, and the put would be $3.98. So, in other words, Vega tells you how much the price of the options increases for every 1 point increase in implied volatility. The closer you get to the expiration date, the smaller vega gets.

When you are in long positions, vega is positive, and it's negative for short positions.

Rho

Rho is a measure of the options pricing's sensitivity to a change in the risk-free interest rate. Since interest rates don't change by that much or that often these days, rho isn't paid much attention to. In a radically changing high-interest rate environment such as existed in the late 1970s, rho would be a more important parameter to pay attention to.

Black-Scholes Equation

The Black-Scholes equation incorporates the option as a function of the underlying stock price and time, the volatility of the stock, and the risk- free interest rate. The equation tells us that gamma represents the gain from holding an option. The equation gives us the "riskless" returns where gamma offsets theta decay. The Black-Scholes equation involves some pretty advanced mathematics, and those with the interest and skills can look up references if they are interested in getting a deeper understanding of the equation. It is a partial differential equation that can estimate the future price of an option. Most options traders don't have to know about the Black-Scholes equation, however. You can simply use tools like spreadsheets or online models that people have created to put the equation into practice for you, and you can play with the various inputs to estimate the future price moves of options you are interested in investing in. The model led to a Nobel Prize in economics. One important fact is that the model is set to work with European options that can be utilized only on the expiration date, and it does not work with American options. However, there are many mathematical models that work quite well for American options.

CHAPTER 5: ACCURATE TRADING STRATEGIES

We are now going to leave the world of selling options and go back to the one that most people are interested in, which is the world of trading options. We are going to have a look at strategies that can be used to increase the odds of profits when trading options. In reality, some of these strategies involve buying and selling options at the same time. Keep in mind that these techniques will require a higher-level designation from your broker. So, it might not be something you can use right away if you are a beginner.

Strangles

One of the simplest strategies that go beyond simply buying options, hoping to profit on moves of the underlying share price, is called a strangle. This strategy involves buying a call option and a put option simultaneously. They will have the same expiration dates, but different strike prices. If the price of the stock rises the put option will expire worthless (but of course it may still hold a small amount of value when you closed your position, and you can sell it and recoup some of the loss). But you will make a profit off the call option. On the other hand, if the stock price declines, the call option will expire worthlessly, but you can make a profit from the put option.

In this case, you can make substantial profits no matter which way the stock moves, but the larger the move, the more profits. On the upside, the profit potential is theoretically unlimited. On the downside, the stock could theoretically fall to zero, so there is a limit, but potential gains are substantial.

The breakeven price on the upside is the strike price of the call plus the amount of the two premiums settled for the options. If the stock price declines the break-even price would be the difference between the strike value of the put option and the sum of the two premiums paid for the options.

Straddles

When you purchase a call and a put option with similar strike amounts and expiration dates, this is called a straddle. The idea here is that the trader is hoping the share price will either rise or fall by a significant amount. It won't matter which way the price moves. Again, if the price rises the put option will expire worthless, if the price falls the call option will expire worthlessly. For example, suppose a stock is trading at $100 a share. We can buy at the money call and put options that expire in 30 days. The price of the call and put options would be $344 and $342 respectively, for a total investment of $686.

With 20 days left to expiration, suppose the share price rises to $107. Then the call is priced at $766, and the put is at $65. We can sell them both at this time, for $831 and take a profit of $145.

Suppose that, instead of at 20 days to expiration, the share price dropped to $92. In that case, the call is priced at $39, and the put is priced at $837. We can sell them for $876, making a profit of $190.

So, although the profits are modest compared to a situation where we had speculated correctly on the directional move of the stock and bought only calls or puts, this way we profit no matter which way the share price moves. The downside to this strategy is that the share price may not move in a big enough way to make profits possible.

Remember that extrinsic value will be declining for both the call and the put options.

Selling covered calls against LEAPS and other LEAPS Strategies

A LEAP is a long-term option, that is an option that expires at a date that is two years in the future. They are regular options otherwise, but you can do some interesting things with LEAPS. Because the expiration date is so far away, they cost a lot more. Looking at Apple, call options with a $195 strike price that expires in two years are selling for $28.28 (for a total price of $2,828). While that seems expensive, consider that 100 shares of Apple would cost $19,422 at the time of writing.

If you buy in the money LEAPS, then you can use them to sell covered calls. This is an interesting strategy that lets you earn premium income without having actually to buy the shares of stock.

LEAPS can also be used for other investing strategies. For example, if Apple is trading at $194, we can buy a LEAP option for $3,479 with a strike price of $190 that expires in two years. If, at some point during that two-year period, the share price rose to $200 we could exercise the option and buy the shares at $190, saving $10 a share. Also, at the same time, we could have been selling covered calls against the LEAPS.

Buying Put Options as Insurance

A put option gives you the right to sell shares of stock at a certain price. Suppose that you wanted to ensure your investment in Apple stock, and you had purchased 100 shares at $191 a share, for a total investment of $19,000. You are worried that the share price is going to drop and so you could buy a put option as a kind of insurance. Looking ahead, you see a put option with a $190 strike price for $4.10. So, you spend $410 and buy the put option.

Should the price of Apple shares suddenly tumble you could exercise your right under the put option to dispose of your shares by selling at the strike price to minimize your losses. Suppose you wake up one morning and the share price has dropped to $170 for some reason. Had you not bought the option you could have tried to get rid of your shares now and take a loss of $21 a share. But, since you bought the put option, you can sell your shares for $190 a share. That is a $1 loss since you purchased the shares at $191. However, you also have to take into account the premium paid for the put options contract, which was $4.10. So, your total loss would be $5.10 a share, but that is still less than the loss of $21 a share that you would have suffered selling the shares on the market at the $170 price. When investors buy stock and a put at the same time, it is called a married put.

Spreads

Spreads involve buying and selling options simultaneously. This is a more complicated options strategy that is only used by advanced traders. You will have to get a high-level designation with your brokerage in order to use this type of strategy. We won't go into details because these methods are beyond the scope of junior options traders, but we will briefly mention some of the more popular methods so that you can have some awareness.

One of the interesting things about spreads is they can be used by level 3 traders to earn regular income from options. If you think the price of a stock is going to stay the same or rise, you sell a put credit spread. You sell a higher-priced option and buy a lower-priced option at the same time. The difference in option prices is your profit. There is a chance of loss if the price drops to the strike price of the puts (and you could get assigned if it goes below the strike price of the put option you sold). You can buy back the spread, in that case, to avoid getting assigned.

If you think that the price of a stock is going to drop you can sell to open a credit spread. In this case, you are hoping the price of the stock is going to stay the same or drop. You sell a call with a low strike price and buy a call with a high strike price (both out of the money). The difference in price is your profit, and losses are capped.

We can also consider more complicated spreads.

For example, you can use a diagonal spread with calls. This means you buy a call that has a shorter expiration date but a strike amount that is higher, and then you sell a call with a longer expiration date and a lower strike price. This is done in such a way that you earn more, from selling the call, than you spend on buying the call for a considerable strike amount, and so you get a net credit to your account. Spreads can become quite complicated, and there are many different types of spreads. If a trader thinks that the price of a stock will only go up a small amount, they can do bull call. Profit and loss are capped in this case. The two options would have the same expiration date.

If you sell a call with a lower strike price and simultaneously buy a call with a high strike price, this is called a bear call spread. You seek to profit if the underlying stock drops in price. This can also be done by using two put options. In that case, you buy a put option that has a higher strike and sell a put option with a lower strike price.

A bull spread involves attempting to profit when the price of the stock rises by a small amount. In this case, you can also use either two call options or two put options. You buy an option with a lower strike price while selling an option with a higher strike price.

Spreads can be combined in more complicated ways. An iron butterfly combines a bear call spread with a bear put spread. The purpose of doing this is to generate steady income while minimizing the risk of loss.

An iron condor uses a put spread, and a call spread together. There would be four options simultaneously, with the same expiration dates but different strike prices. It involves selling both sides (calls and puts).

Iron Condor

If you think the price of a stock is going to stay within a certain range, you can sell to open an iron condor. This type of strategy requires you to buy a call and sell a call (creating a call credit spread) and buy a put and sell a put (creating a put credit spread). Let's see how it is built in steps. All options in this strategy have the same expiration date.

First, you pick an out of the money call price, a bit above the current share price. You sell this call. Then you buy one with a strike that is a little bit higher. The net difference gives you a credit.

Now you pick an out of the money put option, that is below the current share price. Then you sell this put option. Next, you buy an out of the money put option that has an even lower strike price. The difference here gives you another credit.

The maximum profit is the net credits. The maximum loss is given by (width of strike prices) – entry price. The broker will make you put up enough cash to cover the loss unless you have a margin account.

The narrower you make your strike prices the lower your maximum loss, but the higher the probability that you will experience a loss. The range is set by the two options you sell, you want the stock price to stay within those bounds.

The iron condor is a great strategy to use for monthly income. It can work especially well over short time frames, like a week, since that lessens the chance of the stock going outside the range. However, many traders use a month for their iron condors.

Iron Butterfly

An iron butterfly is another strategy to use if you think the stock price will stay within a certain range. It will use four options, like the iron condor, but there will be three different strike prices.

In this case, you will sell a put option and a call option with the same strike price. The strategy is to get as close to at the money as possible. We will call the strike priced used the central strike. Then you set a differential price we will call x. Now you buy a put option with a strike price of (central strike – x), and you buy a call option with a strike price of (central strike + x).

Like an iron condor, the profit from an iron butterfly is fixed at the net credit when you sell to open. This is given by the sum of the premiums earned from selling the at the money call and put, minus the prices paid for the out of the money options.

The maximum loss is the strike price of the purchased call – strike price of the sold put – total premium.

CHAPTER 6: THE BEST STRATEGIES FOR COVERED CALLS

When you sell or write a covered call, you give away your right to buy a stock you own, at a particular price, and within a stated time. From the sale, you pocket the premium, and this amount acts as a cover for when the stock value increases above your strike price.

As you choose a stock from your portfolio, settle on one that has already performed well, but one that you wouldn't mind giving up if the call option was assigned. Avoid picking stocks that you feel very bullish about in the long-term, and that way, you will not be too discouraged when you have to give up stock and end up not receiving any net returns from your investment.

Once you have settled on a stock, it is time to pick the strike price with which you are comfortable selling the stock. Typically, your strike price should not be out-of-the-money, because the goal is to see the price of your stock rise further before you give it up. You must pick an expiration date also, the date by which your call option will be termed worthless. 30 to 45 days from now would be an excellent starting point but trust your judgment more. Select a date that would allow you to have a decent premium if you sold the option at your chosen strike price.

Do not struggle when deciding on an acceptable premium. Some traders fear that they are either selling themselves short or being greedy. One rule of thumb among investors is that an acceptable premium is one that is approximately 2% of the value of your stock. You must remember that options are sensitive to time decay. Therefore, the further you go in time, the more valuable your call option will be. However, going so far in time will make it harder to predict the market trends, and the investors will be apprehensive about taking up your options.

As you will realize in your consecutive trades, the time value is a good indicator of the viability of an option. If you notice that a premium is abnormally high, there must be an underlying sensitive reason behind it. Go on into the market and find out. Search for information in the news also, and find out what could be affective the stock price. Most times, when something looks too promising, it is.

The Three Possible Outcomes of Writing Your Covered Call Options

Your sale of covered call options could produce three different outcomes:

The Stock Price Could Go Down

If after the sale, at the time the option expires, the stock has gone down, your call option will expire worthless. The good news is that you get to keep the entire premium you received when you sold it. The bad news, however, is that the value of your stocks will be down. When the stock price is down, the risk lies in the stocks, not the options part. However, the profit you got when you kept the premium will help offset the value loss.

If the stock price falls before the options expire, do not worry. The fall will not lock you into your position. Although you will have lost in terms of the value of your stock, the value of the call option you sold will have fallen too. This is not bad at all because you now have the opportunity to buy back your option for less than you were paid for it. If you no longer fancy the option on your stock, just close your stock by buying back the low-priced option you sold and get rid of the stock.

The Stock Price Could Go Above the Strike Price

If the stock price goes above the strike price on the day of expiration, the call option will be assigned to you, and you will have to give up 100 shares from your stock. If the value of the stock now rises again after you have given up your shares, too bad for you because you will miss the gains from the price rise. You will have already committed yourself, on the basis of your conscious decision to part with the stock at the strike price. When this happens, dust yourself and move on, promising that you will make a better decision next time.

The Stock Price Remains the Same

In this scenario, the price of the stock could remain as is, or rise just a tiny bit. This is not a bad situation because the call option you sold will expire, and you get to keep all the money you received as premium. The underlying stock might also give you a few dollars as returns. Be happy that you get to keep your returns and your stock.

Here's a summary of the strategy for picking and selling call options as described above:

• Pick a low volatile stock

• Buy call options when in-the-money

• Sell your call option when out-of-the-money Assignment to Sellers of Call Options

If a purchaser selects to exercise the option, your shares of stock might be collected from you, as we mentioned above. We use the word 'might' because it is not guaranteed that you would be asked to deliver your shares; it all depends on whether you are assigned.

The assignment process works through a random lottery system that the Options Clearing Corporation (OCC) runs. When an exercise notice gets to the OCC, the OCC assigns it to a member clearing firm, the brokerage. The brokerage then assigns exercise notices randomly to various short options in their books. You may or may not be assigned. It is possible that you will escape the assignment. However, if the call option is in-the-money, with more than a few cents, the likelihood of escaping this assignment is very low. In all this, whether the option is out-of-the-money or in-the- money, the call buyer retains the right to exercise or not to exercise his option at any time before the expiration, whether it makes sense or not.

Tips for Selling Covered Options Think About the Volatility

It is best to take up the covered call strategy when dealing with stocks that exhibit medium implied volatility. For this, you will want to choose a stock that can move, but in a sort of predictable direction. If the implied volatility is low, don't expect to get much in terms of the premium. If the implied volatility is high, you will have the pleasure of getting higher premiums.

Unfortunately, when the volatility of the stock is high, the stock price could go either way, significantly. If the prices increase, your chances of having your stock called away increases, but if the stock price drops sharply, you stand to make a significant loss. Once the price rises too high and the buyer exercises his option so that your stock is called, you cease to be a stockholder, assuming you had traded in options for that represent all your shares.

As you see, neither of the extremes is good; it is best to work with medium volatility because it will make getting the premium for the call you write worthwhile. It also brings down the unpredictability that comes with high volatility. Therefore, be wise in choosing the premium amount that will make the strategy you have taken worthwhile.

If assigned, Do Not Panic

If what you dreaded comes to be and you are called to give up your stock, it may be surprising and upsetting to have to give up a long-held stock position. Luckily, in that situation, you have more choices than you know.

Suppose you have continually invested in Company G's shares, 100 shares each year, over the past 10 years, and each year, the price was higher than the price in the past year. It then happens that you write one covered call that goes against your holdings.

If you are assigned, you get to choose the lot of shares you want to give up from the lots you have been accumulating over the years. It would serve you better to give up the most expensive of them, the ones you bought the latest, and to keep the less expensive ones you purchased earlier. By doing this, you will have avoided triggering a large tax bill that is charged on the capital gains of your stock. However, when this time comes, ensure that you seek the help and advice of your tax professional.

If you hold your stock close and are not willing to let any of it go, that is still okay. Instead, head on to the open market, buy stock on the margin and deliver it instead. When you do this, you will have better control of your long-term stock positions and of the tax consequences that will come up.

However, keep in mind that if you choose to deliver the newly purchased shares, you will need to have anticipated your assignment so that you buy the new shares before the assignment notice.

It is also true that purchasing on-the-margin stock carries its own risks. Essentially, the margin is a line of credit for purchasing stock for which a trader makes a down payment and pays the broker an interest rate. Trading by this margin is risky because if suddenly the market moves against you, you will be required to add more money to the down payment you made, in what is called a margin call.

Think of Buy-Writes

Some people use covered calls to make some consistent income. They buy the stock then sell the call option in a bid to make some money, all in one transaction. This strategy is called the buy-write.

A buy-write offers many benefits. For one, it is convenient because the trader does not have to head back to the market after making the transaction. The strategy also reduces the trader's market risk by preventing legging. Legging into a trade is getting into a multi-leg options trading position by getting into more than one transaction. Since a lot can happen as the trader moves from one trade to the next, even when they are just a few minutes apart, legging can happen, and it complicates the situation while adding onto the risks to which a trader is exposed.

As such, allowing yourself to get into a multi-leg position can be quite tricky. Most of the time, traders have to pay two commissions and go through tough tax treatment, which depends on each individual's situation. However, before you take up a buy-write, consult a tax advisor.

Come Up with a Plan for When the Situation Turns Against You

If you are bullish about a stock, in the long-term, you would typically write a covered call. However, this call too, can go south, and you will need a plan to control the damage. Unlike what people believe, in this situation too, you will have a number of choices from which to choose.

Unlike what many investors assume, selling your call does not limit you to one position up until the call expires; you could always buy back your call and take away your obligation to give up your stock. We have mentioned this already.

The situation is different if you realize that the price of the stock has fallen since you sold the call. You might have the opportunity to purchase your call back, although this will be at a price lower than the initial sale price. Doing this will allow you to make a profit on your position.

If you want, you can also dump your long stock position, and this will prevent further losses, particularly if the stock continues to drop.

Make a Comparison Between If-Called and Static Returns

Covered calls are a smart way to earn an income out of your long stock positions beside the dividends that the company's payout to shareholders. The if-called and static returns enable you to figure out whether selling your call would be a smart move for your investment plan.

Static returns refer to the scenario where your covered call and the stock do not budge, giving you the right to keep the premium paid as part of your income. The if-called return assumes that you will be assigned and that you will have to give up your stock.

Before you take up the covered call strategy, ensure that you consider both scenarios described above. The numbers therein are important because they will ensure that you continually work towards reaching your investment goals. When you do this, you will be happy with your investment returns and whichever way the situation turns out.

Mistakes Investors Make When Selling Covered Calls

Factors like unpredictable markets often lead investors to make mistakes in their quest to build a profitable portfolio. Here are some of the mistake's traders make:

Selling Their Options Naked Rather Than Covered In the case of covered calls, the premium marks the maximum profit a trader could receive. If the value of the underlying asset significantly increases, and the investor does not own stock of the underlying asset, the investor could suffer high losses. A call option without an underlying stock is called a naked call, and it is very risky because its upside potential is limited while its downside potential is unlimited.

As such, investors must purchase shares on the underlying stock before the option expires. Depending on the underlying stock's market cost, buying the stock could dig a large hole in your capital and end up in losses. Therefore, if an investor wants to take up the covered call strategy, he should mainly focus on selling covered calls on stocks he or she already owns or can afford to purchase. Selling at Expiration or at the Wrong Strike Price One of the critical trading mistakes options traders make is to sell the calls on the day they expire, or at the wrong strike price, having not fully understood the rewards and the risks that come with each move.

The strike price greatly influences your profitability. Therefore, when you choose your strike price, first consider your desired payoff, and the amount of risk you are willing to tolerate.

The strike price of an out-of-the-money call will be higher than the present value of the stock, while the strike price of an in-the-money option is less than the market value of the stock. When you sell an in-the-money option, you get to collect more premiums, and you increase your chances of being called away.

The expiration date is also very important. Lately, options expire after a week, a month, a quarter, and a year. A longer dater option gets a greater premium because its time of decay is far off. However, call sellers benefit more from shorter-term options.

Failing to Have A Loss-Management Plan

Most traders are not prepared for the reality that the trade could very well move against even their best predictions.

Although no one goes into a trade hoping that it will go wrong, you should be ready for this possibility, and take measures to manage the risks that come with that.

Primarily, a plan to manage losses involves having an outlay of the money you are willing to risk in your trade even before you enter a position. You also should know how you will bail out of a trade if it goes the other way, so you may have a definite plan to help you cut your losses.

As you make your plans, it also makes sense to have a realistic picture of the profit you will be targeting. This, you will gauge by looking at the historical movement of your underlying asset, and you should leave enough room to wiggle should the market become unstable, and the stock prices start to fall or rise drastically.

Be careful that there isn't one loss-cutting strategy that will suit all trading scenarios; each trading style will need a new damage control strategy. Besides your style of trading, the size of your account and the position size will also matter.

The advantage is that when trading options, you get great flexibility. For instance, you may opt to buy back your option to relinquish your obligation to deliver your stock.

Only remember that when you notice that a trade is moving against you, the best strategy is not to add more money to it, stick to what you were doing and accept the loss. Keeping your emotions in check is critical in financial trading.

Failing to Factor in the Dividends

Dividends are an important consideration when it comes to evaluating option prices in your quest to choose the right stock. If you buy

100 shares, you will receive dividend payments if the company makes them out, so long as the ex-date comes before the day the contract expires. This is besides the premium you will receive when you sell your call option.

Undoubtedly, dividend payments will affect the call premium. The dividend payment causes the stock price to fall, and as such, the call premiums fall too, although the put premiums become higher. Therefore, if you are expecting dividend payments, it is better to exercise your call option early.

Expecting Returns Immediately

Options are not necessarily a short-term investment strategy; traders can also use them for long-haul investments. However, when they do this, they should not expect immediate returns. Options can be quite profitable, but they are by no means a 'get-rich-quick' strategy. Realizing the returns you want takes time. Realistically, traders should aim for 10 to 12 percent annual returns.

In addition, traders should have a plan that caters to the possibility of receiving lower returns than what they had expected. However, for the most part, they ought to have a consistent strategy, one that will produce consistent returns for the coming years.

CHAPTER 7: PURCHASE OF CALLS

Buying calls is a more advanced form of training than selling covered calls. But it's not that complicated, so let's dive in. What you're actually buying

Remember that one option contract is for 100 shares, so you'll need to be able to buy 100 shares of the stock in order to exercise your right to buy.

Also, remember that an options contract has a deadline. If the stock price fails to exceed the strike price by the deadline, you're out of luck and will lose whatever money that you invested in the premium. In relative terms, the premium price will be small so chances are if you are careful and not starting out by buying large numbers of options contracts, you won't be out that much money.

Your Goal Buying Options Contracts

The goal when purchasing options contracts is to buy a stock at a price that is lower than its current market value. In other words, you want the stock price to be significantly higher than the strike price so that you're enjoying significant savings in purchasing the stock. When evaluating your options, you'll need to take into account the added costs of the premium paid plus commissions. In some cases, commissions can be substantial so make sure you know what they are ahead of time so that you choose a good strike price and exercise your options at the right time.

You're a trader, not an investor

You may be mentally conditioned to think in terms of investing. An investor wants to build a diversified portfolio over a long time period that they believe will increase in value over the long term. A trader operates in the same universe but has different goals. You are after short term profits – not investments. You are not going to hold this stock. If you were interested in holding the stock, you would simply buy it at the lower price that is currently on offer. Your goal is to be able to buy at the strike price when the stock has increased significantly in price and then sell it immediately so that you can pocket the profits.

Let's take an example. Suppose that XYZ corporation is currently selling at $30 a share. People are expecting the stock to rise, and some people are really bullish about its short-term prospects. If you are an investor, your goal is to get the stock at the lowest possible price and then hold it long term. If you are using strategies like dollar cost averaging, you might be buying a few shares every month without paying too much attention to what the price is specifically on the day you purchase. In any case, as an investor, you'll simply buy the shares at $30.

As a trader, you're hoping to cash in on the moves of XYZ over the next couple of months. You'll buy an options contract, let's say its premium is $0.90 and the strike price is $35. Your cost for the 100 shares is $90.

Then the stock price shoots up to $45. Since it passed the strike price, you can exercise your option to buy the shares at the strike price. You can buy them at $35 for a total price of $3,500. But remember – you're not an investor in for the long haul. You'll immediately unload the shares. You sell the shares for $4,500 and make a $1,000 profit. After considering your premium, your profit is $910. It will go a little bit lower after considering commissions, but you get the idea. The purpose of buying call options is to make fast profits on stocks you think are going to spike.

It's hard to guess when the best time is to really buy call options. Obviously, you don't want to do it when a major recession hit. The optimal time is during a bull market, or when a specific company is expected to hit on something big, that will suddenly increase its value in the markets. A good time to look is also when a recession hits, but it passes the bottom out period.

Benefits of Buying Call Options

Call options have many benefits that we've already touched on earlier.

In Particular:

• Call options allow you to control 100 shares of stock without actually investing in the 100 shares – unless they reach a price where you get the profit that you want.

• Call options allow you to sit and wait, patiently watching the market

before making your move.

• If your bet doesn't work out, you're only going to lose a small amount of money on the contract. In our example, if XYZ loses value, and ends up at $28 per share instead of moving past your strike price of $35, then you're only out the $90 you paid for the premium.

• Call buying provides a way to leverage expensive stock.

What to look for when buying Call options

Now let's take a look at some factors that you'll be on the lookout for when buying call options. You're going to want to be able to purchase shares of the stock you're interested in at a price that is less than the price you think it will go up to. You need to do this in order to ensure that the stock price surpasses the strike price. Of course, it's impossible to know what the future holds so this will involve a bit of speculation. You'll have to do a lot of reading and research to make educated guesses on where you expect the stock to go in the next few weeks or months.

Second, you'll need to take into account the cost of the premium when making your estimates. For the sake of simplicity, suppose that you find a call option with a premium of $1 per share. You're going to need a strike price that is high enough to take that into account. If you go for a stock that is $40 a share with a $1 premium and a strike price of $41, obviously you're not going to make anything unless the stock price goes

higher than $41.

Remember that exercising your rights on the options contract is not a path toward immediate money. You're going to have to turn around and sell it ASAP in order to profit. Of course, when you sell is a judgment call as is when you exercise your right to buy. You're going to want to wait until the right moment to buy, but its impossible to really know what that right moment is. This is where trading experience helps and even then, the most skilled experts can make mistakes. For a beginner, the best thing to do is exercise your right to buy the shares and then sell them as soon as they've gone far enough past the strike price for you to make a profit and cover the premium. If you wait too long, there is always the chance that the stock price will start declining again, and it will go below your strike price and never exceed it again before the contract expires.

Open Interest

If you get online to check stocks you're interested in, one of the measures you will see is "Open Interest." This tells you the number of open or outstanding derivative contracts there are for that particular stock. Every time that a buyer and seller enter into an options contract, this value increases by one. What you want to do with open interest as a trader looking to make real cash from call options is to look for stocks that show big movement in the number of open trades. You're going to want to look for increasing numbers. This means that other traders have an interest in buying call options on this stock and that they're expecting it to go up in value in the near future.

Of course, you're going to want to take an educated approach to this. Simply getting online and going through random stocks will be a waste of time, it might take you weeks to find something.

You're going to want to prepare ahead of time by keeping an eye on the financial news. Watch Fox Business, read the Wall Street Journal, and watch CNBC and read any other financial publications that are to your liking. Find out what stocks the experts are talking about and which ones they expect to make significant moves over the next few weeks and months. Keep in mind these people and experts often make mistakes, so you're only using it as a guideline. You also don't want to focus solely on looking for stocks that are going to make moves; you want to keep up with company news. You need to keep your ears open for news such as the development of a new drug or the latest electronic gadget. Sometimes you might find out news about that before the stock begins attracting a lot of interest in the markets.

Tips for Buying Call Options

• Don't buy a call option with a strike price that you don't think the stock can beat.

• Always include the premium price in your analysis.

• Look for calls that are just in the money. These are likely to bring a modest profit.

• Call options that are out of the money might give you an option for a cheaper premium.

• However, the premium shouldn't be your primary consideration when looking to buy a call option. Compared to the money required to buy the shares and the potential profits if the stock goes past the strike price, the premium is going to be a trivial cost in most cases – provided of course the strike price is high enough to take the premium into account.

• Look at the time value. If you're looking for larger profits, it's better to aim for longer contracts. Remember, that with any call option you have the option to buy the stock at the strike price at any time between today's date and the deadline when the stock market price exceeds the strike price. Longer time frames mean you increase the chances of that happening. Even if the price goes a little above the strike price and dips down, with a longer window of time before the deadline, you can wait and see if it rebounds. Remember if it never does, you're only out the

premium.

• Start small. Beginning traders shouldn't bet the farm on options. You'll end up broke if you do that. The better approach is to start by investing in one contract at a time and gaining experience as you go.

CHAPTER 8: PUT OPTION

Puts, of course, allow you to sell the stock that you have or the underlying commodity that you have underneath it all. There are different reasons why people may want to buy or sell puts, and here we'll go over what it is, how to do it, and the advantages of such. What is Buying and Selling Puts?

Selling/buying puts essentially is giving someone the option to buy the stock at a certain amount of money.

If you sell a put option, you're selling the chance for someone to buy that stock at a price.

If you buy a put option, you're giving someone the option to buy that stock for that price and the person is obligated to sell it.

So, let's say that you're planning on getting a put option to buy that stock at a certain amount of money. You can put that option down, and from there, wait for it to fall, and from there you can exercise it. Maybe you want to buy shares from a really good railroad company. You essentially notice it's increasing the earnings on this, and you decide to potentially buy the stock when it's under 30. By buying a put option, it basically makes the seller obligated to sell you the stock when it falls below 30 dollars.

You want to exercise these in falling markets since you'll generate a profit when the market is falling, rather than rising. Selling Puts in this Market

Here's the thing, when you want to sell puts, you should only do so if you're comfy with the owning stock that's under it at the price that's there because essentially, you're assuming the obligation to buy it if the person does decide to sell. From this, you should also only enter trades where the net price paid for the security is good. This is the most important part of selling puts profitably in the markets that you have. There are other reasons to sell it to the person. You also can own the security below the market price that is currently there, and you'll definitely want to be careful when you do choose to sell this.

An Example of Buying a Put

Let us now move onto buying these puts. One thing to note is that you're not going to see the commissions, taxes, margins, and other charges factored into any of these equations for a reason. That starts to get it a bit more complicated, and right now, we are just showing you the cut and dry of all of the ways you can buy a put option that can be considered. But, you should definitely consult with your tax advisor or broker before you go in.

Put options essentially give you that right to sell it at a certain price by a time period. You essentially pay the premium, which will from there will sell you that stock at that price.

So let's say you've got company A, which is overvalued currently at $50 bucks a share, and you decide to bet on a decline at this point, getting a put contract that's at $35 a share, and it costs $2 per share, so the "breakeven" price is $33 a share. This is deduced from basic math, since you're taking the contract price of 35 minus the 2 making it $33 for this. Since each of these represents 100 different shares. That's $3500 in total of what you'll buy, and then of course it'll cost you upfront $200 for this (cause of the options contract and the shares) and from there, you enter the trade.

So the best time to use these is when you have a sinking ship in terms of stock. Otherwise, they aren't worth your time, and it's better to not have these stocks, and there is always a chance you could end up losing money. But, if the person sells the stock, and you turn around and cash in on it, you'll have more money, and you don't have to worry about the burden of a stock.

If you choose to buy it when it declines, you're essentially going to get money from this. You want to do it when it's declining and nothing more. It is very important that you don't choose to act on these types of options until it's that time.

That's it, that's all buying put options is, and you want to make sure that it falls to the level that you want it to be at.

The risks of it

Risks are still there in both cases. Options are risky due to the complex nature of this, but once you know how these works, it can reduce the risk a whole lot. Put options, in particular, can be quite risky, especially for the seller, since they may have to spend more money buying back the option that they once had.

One other aspect of this, especially for buyers is the break-even aspects of it. So, let's assume that you got a stock today for $46 and this was at $44, which is two points down what it is there, so you'll be profitable in the trade. But, here's the thing, you're going end up losing out on money due to the fee for the option. It would make the option worth $2 since you spent $4 on it, so that means you're losing out on it.

But there is also the fact that if the option does expire and you're in-the- money, you'll get the right stock immediately. You may not realize it, but these can be quite good, especially for plunging markets, especially if you know they will bounce back.

If you end up seeing it go high, you're going to end up paying for that premium to get the right to buy it, and that's money that can rack up to a couple of thousand dollars. Do make sure that you understand that when you do choose to figure out your own stock, and how you can easily rectify.

The Advantages of Buying Puts

Buying puts, which gives you an option to sell the stock at a given price, is good if you're looking to protect yourself. So let's say that you have this stock, or you've been eyeing a stock that will probably fall, and then rise over the next few months. There are those out there, and usually, it's due to lulls in the market at the time. So, you decide to buy the put that's there, which gives you the option to sell that stock when the market decides to resurface at a higher level.

For you, you're taking a gamble on this, because the market may not recover, but if you notice a stock that could potentially have the power to possibly fall, this may be a good one. That way, you can get the stock for cheaper. From there, you can sell the stock again, and you have the right to sell that stock at the price that you're looking for.

It essentially allows you to form that extra security in his, which is a nice little advantage for the person who wants to sell it. Long puts are good for this, especially if you want to sell these.

Put options let you sell this asset at the strike price that's there. With this, the seller is then obligated to purchase these shares from the holder. Now, how can this help? Let's say that you buy a stock at 20 bucks, and then you compare it to 20 dollars at the edge that's there. If the price is below 20 at any point, you can actually then exercise the options and reduce the losses. This can definitely help, especially if you're willing to buy an option, and from there, sell it in order to avoid lots of trouble.

Naked Puts

There are also naked puts, which is an advanced put options strategy, so I don't suggest trying this till you've worked with basic puts. The reason for that is because of their incredibly risky.

What does it mean to trade an option naked though? It doesn't mean that you're going to the stock exchange in the buff, but rather, you're selling the options without having a position in the underlying instrument. For example, if you're writing a naked put, you're selling a put without having the stock.

The covered call is probably the most basic stock trading strategy. This strategy provides an ideal entry point for those who are new to options trading and allows them to turn their existing investment activities into a gateway for trading options. The premise of the covered call is quite simple. The idea behind this strategy is to minimize your cost basis on your stock purchases.

CHAPTER 9: THE VARIOUS SPREAD STRATEGIES

When it comes to spread trading, there are two categories all types of trades fit into. These are vertical spreads and horizontal spreads. The names sound fancy but understanding how they work really isn't anywhere near as complicated.

Having said that, these types of trades do crank the complexity level up a bit. If the collar took things up a notch from covered calls then spread trades do the same with the collar. As beneficial as collars and covered calls are there is one major disadvantage that those strategies pose to the trader.

They require a long stock purchase. In the case of a covered call this is an investment while in the case of a collar it can be speculative or an investment. Whatever the designation there's no escaping the fact that long stock investment requires a lot of money. What if you wish to emulate Thales' example and get in on low capital values?

This is what the spread strategies address. Options give us the flexibility to play around with the way price moves and as you'll see, spread trades encompass taking advantage of a wide variety of market behavior.

Bull Call Spreads

The first type of vertical spread we'll be looking at is the bull call spread. This is a bullish trading strategy and works best in the middle portions of trending markets. I'll address why this is so. For now keep in mind that while this is a bullish strategy it works best when bullishness is beginning to slow down and you observe the ranges getting larger.

You can utilize this in the earlier, more forceful, part of trends but this isn't the most efficient use of it. In those portions, you're better off simply buying a call and letting its premium rise. The covered call works well in those environments too.

Either way, the bull call spread has two legs to it. You will be buying one call and selling another. Thus the long call leg of the trade covers the short call. Let's take a look at the legs in more details

Trade Legs

The first leg you should establish is the long call leg. This needs to be an at the money or sightly out of the money call that you're sure will move into the money soon. The objective is to use this leg to make the majority of the profit in this trade. In essence, you're substituting the long stock position from the prior two strategies with a long call position.

Establishing a long stock position meant that you needed to protect it somehow which is why we had to incorporate a third leg in the case of the collar. With the covered call, given the investment nature of the trade, downside protection is moot since you'll be holding onto it for the long term anyway and the objective is to hold onto your investment no matter how much it dips (assuming the dip isn't catastrophic.)

The second leg of the bull call spread is the short call. This is written out of the money at a point where you think price will advance to, even if it does so sluggishly. Much like with every other strategy we've looked at, you want both of these options to expire at least 30 days or more from the trade date. This helps you capture and avoid the risk of time decay.

Like the collar, the bull call spread can be adjusted and its greatest power lies in a good adjustment. This allows you to remain in the market at low cost. Adjustments depend on what the market scenario looks like. As I mentioned earlier, you should deploy this in times when bullishness is starting to be challenged by bearishness and thus, you will enter with the knowledge that the trend is still strong but there are some headwinds ahead.

You should place your short call at a level beyond the most relevant resistance ahead. Once price breaches this level, you should move it a few points higher to where the next resistance level could potentially be and so on. Alternatively, if you feel that the counter trend presence is becoming far too much, you could let the market take you out of the position and close your long and cover your short position.

Bull Put Spread

The bull put spread strategy seeks to take advantage of the exact same set of market conditions that the bull call spread seeks. So what is the difference between the two? Aside from the obvious fact that one strategy uses calls and the other uses puts, there are many subtleties that you ought to be aware of.

The strategies do not contradict one another, in case you're wondering. Think of it as having two choices to pursue depending on what market conditions look like. If you're wondering how to determine the conditions which are ideal for each strategy, then the first step is to take a look at the bull put spread and understand how it works.

Trade Legs

Like the bull call, the bull put is a two legged trade. The first leg involves establishing a long put position which is out of the money and is below a strong support level. This long put is what caps your downside risk in case things go wrong. In addition to this, the long put also covers the next leg.

This is a short put which is written near or at the money. This leg is the primary profit driving instrument for the trade. I'd like to point out here that the structure and positioning of the puts is very different from that of the calls. With the bull call spread, you were capping your maximum gain on the trade by writing an OTM call.

Here's you're not capping any gains and are in fact capping your loss via a trade leg. In the bull call spread, your maximum loss was automatically capped as a part of the trade structure. You could argue that this is what is happening here as well but it's pretty clear that the way in which the strategies do this is very different.

The next major point of difference is in the results trade entry gives you. The bull call is net debit trade but the bull put is a net credit trade. Net debit trades have you realize your maximum loss upon trade entry. Net credit trades realize your maximum gain upon entry. This means, you earn your maximum profit on entry and if all goes well, your options will maintain themselves.

Like the bull call spread, you can adjust the trade depending on market conditions. Given that your upside is not capped, adjustments will need to be made primarily if the market turns downwards and if you see your puts move into the money. In this case, you will need to readjust the spread lower and exit your primary position. Thus, the adjustment scenarios in the bull put strategy aren't as varied as they are in the others we've seen so far.

If the trade works in your favor, you can establish a higher spread using the same principles you used to establish the initial one. Let's take a look at an example and see how the trade works.

Bear Call Spread

If you can use call spreads to take advantage of bullish conditions, you can use them to take advantage of bearish ones as well. In case you're wondering, it is possible to do this with puts as well and much like what we saw with the bullish spreads, you have a choice of using either call or put spreads to do this.

The bear call spread has two legs to it, much like the bull spreads do. As the name suggests you'll be setting up calls as part of this strategy. Let's take a deeper look at the two legs now.

Trade Legs

The first leg you want to establish is a long call position. The long call is placed at a level that is beyond a resistance zone and is the leg that limits your risk. The call itself is placed out of the money. The further away the call is, the greater your risk in the trade is.

The second leg to establish is the primary profit driving leg of this trade. This is a short call you will write as close to the money as possible. The exact placement of this level is a tricky thing since you don't want it to move into the money. If it does, you'll have to wind up both legs of the trade and take your maximum loss amount.

Bear call spreads are net credit trades which means you'll capture your entire gain upon trade entry. As such, like other options trading strategies we've seen thus far, you don't need to do anything special to maintain the trade. You can adjust it as well but given that this is a net credit trade, there isn't much you can do in terms of adjustment beyond working out another spread level in case the original trade doesn't work out.

Bear Put Spread

The bear put spread is the bearish cousin of the bull call spread in that it is a net debit trade that seeks to capture more of the upside in a bearish movement. By now, hopefully you've got a hang of how vertical spread trades are setup so let's quickly run through how this trade works.

Like the other three it has two legs to it: A long put and a short put.

The long put is established at the money or as near to the money as possible and is the primary profit driver in this trade. The short put is written out of the money, a few levels below and functions as a profit target of sorts.

The aim with this trade, like with the bull call spread is to capture as much of the market movement as possible. Hence, adjustments play an important role here. Once the market moves close to your short call, you can adjust your target downwards and move your long call leg up.

The timeline for this trade is the same as that of the others. You're looking at establishing options that are at least 30 days or so away from the trade entry date in order to avoid or capture as much of the time decay as possible. Using our TSLA example with a market price of $478.15, let's assume that we write the TSLA 450 option expiring a month from now.

This will net us $23.90 in premiums. We can go long on the 475 put which will cost us $36.05. Thus the net debit on the trade and our maximum loss is $12.15. Our maximum gain is limited to the strike price of the OTM put and this is $25.

Horizontal Spreads

Horizontal spreads, like their vertical cousins, are two legged trades. They're easy to setup but can be a bit tricky to analyze prior to entry. This is because most horizontal spreads have a time factor that makes them confusing to some people. All in all, the horizontal spread strategy is one which relies on a little bit of luck.

However, the times you do get it right makes it all worthwhile since the rewards tend to be higher when done well.

Call Calendar Spread

Horizontal spread trades are also called calendar spreads due to the way the two legs of the trade are setup. The call calendar spread is best used after the initial part of an uptrend when the trend begins to slow down. The best part of the calendar spread is that you can set pretty much any time frame you want the trade to work out in.

The first leg to establish is a long call position which has an expiry date at least 60 days out from the trade date. The second leg is a short call position which has an expiration of at least 30 days. The key thing to note is that the long call should expire after the short call does. The strike prices of both calls are the same.

You can see where the term horizontal or calendar comes from. Vertical spreads had you placing trades on calls and puts in the same expiration month but at different strike prices. Here, we're looking at the same strike price but with different expiration dates. This pushes the trade out horizontally.

You can choose an expiration for the long call to be greater than 60 days or even 90 days away. Similarly, you can shorten the time frame for the short call as well but remember that if you move within the 30 day period, time decay means you'll receive less of a premium upon writing the option.

Should you lengthen the time frame of the short call? You an but this is a risky thing to do as you'll see now.

Trade Premise

The idea behind a horizontal call spread is to essentially have you cake and eat it too. Uptrends can sometimes be sluggish. They can be long and drawn out and they can move sideways for long periods of time without losing any strength. This kind of behavior makes a short term vertical spread unprofitable.

Imagine initiating a bull call spread knowing that price is going to move upwards for a long time but as time goes by, price simply sits there. All the while, your vertical spread trade doesn't do anything and you end up paying money to enter the trade. You could initiate a bull put spread but this seems like the wrong thing to do.

What I mean is that if you know that the trend is going to last for a long time, why would you limit your profit right upon entry? It doesn't make sense. This is where a horizontal trade makes far more sense since you can take advantage of both the short term sluggishness as well as the long term potential.

In technical terms, you will see such an opportunity in a trend where counter trend presence has grown and ranges are lasting for a few weeks at a time. In such conditions, the short call (which has a closer expiry date) will help you capture the premium since price is unlikely to hit it. Once price breaks out of the range and moves upwards, the long call will move into the money and you'll be able to capture the profit from the bull move.

Determining the correct strike price when it comes to horizontal trades is even more important than in vertical spreads. Thankfully, it isn't as difficult as it sounds. You need to look at the upcoming resistance levels and choose a price beyond it. Take care to not choose a level that is far too strong. Ideally, you want a level that is medium in strength and is going to hold for at least a month or so.

Using TSLA as an example (market price $478.15,) let's assume $500 to be our ideal strike price. The 500 call expiring a month later will cost us $28.50. The 500 call expiring in 31 days will net us a premium of $20, making this a net debit trade to the tune of $8.50. The ideal scenario would be if TSLA were to stay below 500 for a month or so and then rise past it which will ensure both legs behave appropriately.

If the trade doesn't quite go how you want, you can adjust it to another strategy. Let's say TSLA looks like it will burst past 500 in the current month. At this point, you can adjust the trade to a bull call spread. You can cover your short call position and open another one expiring in the same month as the long call.

Similarly, if TSLA declines sharply and looks like it won't move past 500 anytime soon, you can adjust the trade to be a bear call spread. It depends on how you read the existing market conditions.

Put Calendar Spread

The horizontal put spread is similar in premise to the call calendar spread except it seeks to take advantage of a bearish market. The structure of the trade is also similar to call. It's just that you'll be buying puts instead of calls. There are two legs that are a part of the trade.

The short put leg is placed at a strike price that is beyond a support level that is medium in strength. It will have an expiry date that is beyond 30 days out but less than the expiry date of the second, long put leg. The long put will have the same strike price as the short put.

The idea is to capture the benefits of the short term neutral behavior and the long term bearishness. The shorter term, short put provides a premium and the long term put provides capital gains in the form of increases in intrinsic value as prices dive. This is also a net debit trade.

Much like the call calendar spread, the put spread can be adjusted as well depending on the type of market behavior observed. The most common adjustment methods involve converting it into a vertical spread to take advantage of price behavior.

This concludes our look at horizontal spread trades. As you can see, they're not very complex in nature and are far easier to maintain and understand than vertical spread trades. Spread trades are a step up from collars and like the collar, they offer decent and steady rewards when executed correctly.

CHAPTER 10: CALENDAR DISSEMINATION STRATEGY

Calendar spreads are a strategy that I enjoy trading because it gives traders a special advantage of options: the decline in fair value. Also, this strategy can generate profits, even if the underlying stock is not moving. Calendar spreads belong in the toolbox of a trader who wants to make money even in motionless markets. It has the thrill of the clock ticking, to your advantage emotion to it. In the options jargon, the calendar spread is also sometimes called the time spread or horizontal spread.

For the horizontal or calendar spread, you use the same underlying and the same exercise price. However, you choose different months for the sale and purchase of the option and try to benefit from the volatility of the underlying. With this strategy, the investor speculates that the volatility of the underlying will increase over the term of the option.

Building a calendar spread

The calendar spread strategy consists of short sale of a put option and the purchase of a put option with the same base price. The expiry date of the put option sold is closer than the expiry date of the put option purchased. The calendar spread summarized:

•Short put with strike price A and near expiry date

• Long put with strike price A and later expiry date

• The share price is usually at or above the base price A

Calendar Spread Profile: Principle of a calendar spread

When you run a calendar spread with put options, you take advantage of a special property of options in your favor: the fall in fair value. Since the expiry date of the put option sold is nearer, its expiry time will be faster than the expiry date of the put option purchased, which has a longer-term. Shortly before the expiry date of the short-term put option sold, you want to buy it back as cheaply as possible. At the same time, you sell the longer-term put option to close your position completely. Ideally, the longer-term put option still has a significant fair value.

If you expect the stock to move minimally, trade your calendar spread with put options that are in the money (the stock price is close to the base price of the options). If you expect the stock to decline, trade put options that are out of the money (the stock price is above the base price of the options), since both options have the same base price for a calendar spread, you cannot make a profit from the intrinsic value of the options with the calendar spread: the bought and the sold short options neutralize in this regard. You can only profit from the difference in the current value. However, if the put options slide deep or far out of the money, the time value for both options will gradually disappear.

So you will expect that the share price will stay as close to base price A as possible. With calendar spreads, you can use very different time intervals. The term of the short-term option is typically 3 to 4 weeks, while the longer-term option will have a term of 6 to 9 weeks.

Tips for trading calendar spreads

• For calendar spreads, I prefer to take profits early. If, for example, 10% to 20% of the stake is booked as a profit, you can consider cashing out. This return is typical of a calendar spread that went well. The risk of holding the position until the end (i.e., until the expiry date of the sold option) to squeeze out the last cent is not worth it.

• When closing the position, I recommend closing both options. Don't be tempted to hold the longer-term option in the hope that the stock will move in the desired direction for the remainder of the term.

Who and When is the calendar spread suitable for?

This strategy is intended for traders who already have experience in options trading. The execution of the calendar spread is not particularly complicated, but due to the different terms of the options, it is not as intuitive to grasp as so-called vertical spreads, which only have an expiry date. You open a calendar spread if you expect the stock to stay close to a price within a certain period that corresponds to the base price of the options.

A calendar spread has a lot of variables to determine an exact formula for the profit thresholds. We have to distinguish between the two termination dates of the options; an approximation must be made to "guess" what the value of the long-term put option will be if the short-term put option expires. The performance profile in your trading platform can help you see the initial profit thresholds. However, please note that the displayed performance profile assumes that all other variables, such as implied volatility, remain constant over the entire term of the position, which will not be the case in reality.

Your potential profit is limited to the premium received for the short-term put option sold, less the cost of buying and closing the long-term put option. The maximum profit cannot be determined when the position is opened and depends on the value of the long-term put option on the expiry date of the short-term option. The maximum profit is achieved if, at the end of the term of the short-term option, the share price is quoted as close as possible to the base price A. In this case, the short-term put options sold expire worthlessly, and you sell the long- term put options at their residual value. A partial profit is achieved if the share price remains between the base price A and the profit thresholds. A calendar spread need not be held until the options expire. You can close out the position early and take the profits (or losses) with you.

Examples of a Calendar Spread on Home Depot

If the stock price is exactly $ 215 at the end of the short-term option term, the trader's estimated profit is $ 258. The sold short put option would expire worthless ($ 350 profit), and the purchased put option would be estimated yet 498 $ value. Closing the put option bought would result in a loss of $ 590 - $ 498 = $ 92. Taking into account the $ 350 gain from the short put, the bottom line remains a profit of $ 258. The residual value of the purchased option of $ 498 here is just an assumption that may differ from reality. The position's margin requirement would be to use the trade: $ 240.

The maximum return on the calendar spread would, therefore, be $ 258 / $ 240 = 107.5% in 24 days.

Calendar spreads work well in markets with low volatility. With a calendar spread, you buy a longer-running option, and you write a shorter-running option. For example, you buy 1 AEX FEB 430 Call and go short 1 AEX JAN 430 Call. In this case, you bet on a smooth rise towards 430 points, with the ideal scenario being a January expiration position of 430 points. Then after the January expiration, you still have 1 AEX FEB 430 Call long, which also has sufficient value. In that case, the January call option expires worthless at a level below 430.

With this strategy, you profit from evaporating the time and expectation value of the short-term January option, but the increase should not go too fast. So you have to be careful with fast-moving markets. Bear in mind that if markets move sharply, volatility and therefore also option premiums will rise sharply, which is detrimental to the written options. You will not get the slow movement to the 430.

Calendar spreads that are set up with calls can sometimes work differently because, with a rising market, the panic in the market usually decreases so that the volatility decreases and therefore the option premiums. However, if the market rises very fast, especially at events such as takeovers, volatility can increase.

Calendar spreads are a very special construct in options trading. By combining options with different expiration dates, the "inner workings" of a calendar spread are not always easy to see through. Above all, note that this combination of options benefits greatly from the decline in the fair value of options. If the underlying stock moves little or stays close to its chosen base price, a high percentage of profits will come with the advantage that the risk is limited.

CHAPTER 11: HOW TO CHOOSE THE BEST BROKER

When it comes to selecting brokers, you have many options available. There are full service, discount, online, etc.

Understanding the differences between them and selecting the ones best suited for your purposes is crucial if you wish to succeed. Another area that a lot of beginners ignore and then receive a rude lesson in is the regulations surrounding options trading.

There aren't too many rules to comply with, but they do have significant consequences for your capital and risk strategies.

Choosing a Broker

Generally speaking, there are two major varieties of brokers: Discount and full service. In fact, a lot of full-service brokers have discount arms these days so you will see some overlap. Full service refers to an organization where brokerage is just a part of a larger financial supermarket.

The broker might offer you other investment solutions, estate planning strategies, and so on. They'll also have an in-house research wing which will send you reports to help you trade better. In addition to this, they'll also have phone support in case you have any questions or wish to place an order.

Once you develop a good relationship with them, a full-service broker will become a good organization to network. Every broker loves a profitable customer since it helps with marketing. A full-service broker will have good relationships in the industry and if you have specific needs, they can put you in touch with the right people.

The price of all this service is you paying higher commissions than average. It is up to you to see whether this is a good price for you to pay. As such, you don't need to signup with a full-service broker to trade successfully. Order matching is done electronically so it's not as if a person on the floor can get you a better price these days. Therefore, a full-service house is not going to give you better execution.

Discount brokers, on the other hand, are all about focus. They help you trade, and that is it. They will not provide advice, at least not intentionally from a business perspective, and phone ordering is nonexistent. That doesn't mean customer service is reduced. Far from it.

Commissions will be lower as well, far lower than what you can expect to pay at a full-service house. The downside of a discount brokerage is that you're not going to receive any special product recommendations or solutions outside of your speculative activities. A lot of people prefer to trade (using a separate account) with the broker they have their retirement accounts with so everything is kept in-house.

So which one should you choose? Well, if you aim to keep costs as low as possible, then select a discount broker. In fact, only in the case where you're keen on keeping things in one place should you choose a full- service broker. These days, there's no difference between the two options otherwise.

An exception here is if you have a large amount of capital, north of half a million dollars. In such cases, a full-service broker will be cheaper because of their volume-based commission offers. You'll pay the same rate or as close to what a discount broker would charge you, and you get all the additional services. Whatever additional amounts you need to invest can be handled by the firm through their wealth management line of business.

There are a few terms you must understand, no matter which broker you choose so let's look at these now.

Margin

Margin refers to the number of assets you currently hold in your account. Your assets are cash and positions. As the market value of your positions fluctuates, so does the amount of margin you have. Margin is an important concept to grasp since it is at the core of your risk management discipline.

When you open an account with your broker, you will have a choice to make. You can open either a cash or margin account. In order to trade options, you have to open a margin account. Briefly, a cash account does not include leverage within it, so all you can trade are stocks. There are no account minimums for a cash account, and even if they are, they're pretty minuscule.

A margin account, on the other hand, is subject to very different rules. First, the minimum balances for a margin account are higher. Most brokers will impose a $10,000 minimum, and some will even increase this amount based on your trading style. The account minimum doesn't achieve anything by itself, but it acts as a commitment of sorts for the broker.

The thinking is that with this much money on the line, the person trading is going to be a bit more serious about it and won't blow it away. If only it worked like that. Anyway, the minimum balance is a hard and fast rule. Another rule you should be aware of is the Pattern Day Trader (PDT) designation.

PDT is a rule that comes directly from the SEC. Anyone who executes four or more orders within five days is classified as a PDT ("Pattern Day Trader," 2019). One this tag is slapped onto you, your broker is going to ask you to post at least $25,000 in the margin as a minimum balance. Again, this minimum balance doesn't do anything but the SEC figures that if you do screw up, this gives you enough of a buffer.

Each strategy by itself plays out over a month or more so once you enter, all you need to do is monitor it and if you want, you can adjust it.

However, if you're going to avoid the PDT, you're limited to entering just three positions per workweek.

My advice is to study the strategies and to start slowly. Trade just one instrument at first and see how it goes and then expand once you gain more confidence. At that point, you'll have enough experience to figure out how much capital you need. Remember that even exiting a position is considered a trade, so PDT doesn't refer just to trade entry.

Margin Call

One other aspect of margin you must understand is the margin call. This is a dreaded message for most traders, including institutional ones. The purpose of all risk management is to keep you as far away as possible from this ever happening to you. A margin call is issued when you have inadequate funds in your account to cover its requirements.

Remember that your margin is the combination of the cash you hold plus the value of your positions. If you have $1000 in cash, but your position is currently in a loss of -$900, you'll receive a margin call to post more cash to cover the potential loss you're headed for. In fact, you'll receive it well in advance. If you don't post more margin, your broker has the right to close out your positions and recover whatever cash they can to stop their risk limits from being triggered.

The threshold beyond which your broker will issue a margin call is called the maintenance margin. Usually, you need to maintain 25% of your initial position value (that is when you enter a position) as cash in your account. Most brokers have a handy indicator which tells you how close you are to the limit.

The leading cause of margin calls is leverage. With a margin account, you can borrow money from your broker and use that to boost your returns. Let's look at an example: if you trade with $10,000 of your own money and borrow $20,000 from your broker to enter a position, you control $30,000 worth of the position. Let's say this position makes a gain of $10,000 to bring its total value to $40,000.

You've just made a 100% return on this investment (since you invested just $10,000) despite the total return on the position is 33% (10,000/30,000). What happens if you lose $10,000 on the position though? Well, you just lost 100% despite the position losing only 33%. Leverage is a double-edged sword.

It is far too simplistic to call leverage bad or good. It is what it is. If you're a beginner, you should not be borrowing money to trade under any circumstances. When you're experienced, you can choose to do so as much as you want. Please note, I'm differentiating between the leverage where you borrow money, and the sort of leverage options provide.

With options, a single contract gives you control over a larger pie of stock, but the option premium still needs to be paid. It is, therefore, cheaper to trade options than the common stock. If you were to borrow money to pay for the option premium, then you're indulging in foolish behavior, and you need to step away.

There's a difference between leverage being inherent within the structure of the instrument and using leverage to increase the amount of something you can buy. The latter should be avoided when you're a beginner.

Execution

A favorite pastime of unsuccessful traders is to complain about execution. Their losses are always the broker's fault, and if it weren't for the greedy brokers, they'd be rolling in the dough, diving in and out of it like Scrooge McDuck. Complaining about your execution will get you nothing. A big reason for these complaints is that most beginner traders don't realize that the price they see on the screen is not the same as what is being traded on the exchange.

We live in an era of high-frequency trading, and the markets' smallest measurement of time has gone from seconds to microseconds. Trades are constantly pouring in, and the matching engine is always finding suitable sellers for buyers. Given the pace of the market, it is important to understand that it is humanly impossible to figure out the exact price of an instrument.

Therefore, within your risk management plan, you must make allowance for times of high volatility when the fluctuations will be bigger. For now, I want you to understand that just because the price you received was different from what was on screen doesn't mean the broker is incompetent.

How do you identify an incompetent broker? Customer service and the quality of the trading terminal they give you access to are the best indicators. Your broker is not in the game to trade against you or fleece you. So stop blaming your broker and look at your systems instead, assuming the broker passes basic due diligence.

When it comes to placing orders with your broker, you have many options. There are different order types you can place, and each order has a specific purpose. First off, we have the market order. This is the simplest order to understand. When you place a market order, you're telling your broker to fill your entire order at whatever price they can find on the market.

A market order usually results in fast fills, unless there's a volatility event of some sort going on. The next type of order you can place is the limit order. The limit prioritizes order price over quantity. For example, if you want to enter 100 units of an instrument at $10, your broker will buy as much as possible under or equal to $10. If they can get just 90 units under $10, then that's it.

A limit order works for a lot of traders looking to enter a position. Directional risk management depends a lot on the size of the position, so it is critical not to exceed the positions limit. For such traders, this is a beneficial order. The last type of order you will encounter is the stop order. The stop prioritizes quantity over price.

Stop orders have a trigger attached to them, and once market price hits the trigger, the entire quantity of the order is executed, irrespective of what the price is. Stop orders are very useful to get out of positions quickly. Indeed, the stop-loss order is a stop order with the 'loss' in the name simply referring to the minimization of losses in case the trade goes south.

Another order you should be aware of is the Good Till Cancelled or GTC. A cousin of the GTC is the Day order. These two do not order types as much as expiry conditions for the order. A GTC is valid until the trader explicitly cancels it while the day order cancels itself at the end of the market session.

All in all, there are over a hundred different types of order your average broker offers you. Do not get bogged down trying to figure them all out. Institutional traders use most of them for specific strategies. To trade well, you don't need to understand a single word of what those orders are about. Stick to the ones mentioned here, and you can trade successfully.

The question now is, how and where should you use these orders? Well since you're trading options, you're not going to be too concerned with stop losses and your exits are going to involve letting options expire. Thus, the biggest concern you should have is with regard to trade entry.

With options, you can choose either market or limit orders to enter. Personally, I favor market orders since it guarantees you an entry.

Risk management here is a bit different than with directional trades so you can afford to enter at the market. The only exception is if there are extreme volatility conditions present.

Price Quotes

A lot of traders are stumped when they first look at their trading screens and see that there are two prices for everything. After all, every financial channel always displays one price for security but when trading, you'll be quoted two different prices within the price box. This is a small but crucial detail for you to understand.

The lower price you receive is called the bid, and this is the price you will pay if you sell the instrument. The higher price is the ask, and this is what you will pay to buy the instrument. The single price you see on your TV screen is the "Last Traded Price" or LTP. Do not make the mistake of thinking the LTP is the real price since the market moves constantly.

In fact, even the spread (the difference between the ask and the bid) doesn't accurately reflect the true state of things thanks to constant movement. There's no need to be alarmed though, as long as volatility is stable, the difference isn't much. Just remember to look at the spread to understand what you'll be paying. The spread increases and contracts constantly but if you see that it is getting too big, this is a sign that too much volatility exists and you're better off staying out.

This concludes our look at brokers and the ins and outs of it. As you can see, there isn't too much to be concerned about, but you need to be well aware since it impacts how much capital you'll be trading with. Generally speaking, the higher the capital you have, the safer you'll be since you'll have more room to make mistakes.

Being undercapitalized is one of the biggest reasons traders fail in the markets, so don't make the mistake of jumping in too soon. Also, don't try to get creative with the PDT to the detriment of your strategy. There are several gurus online who will give you 'tricks' and 'hacks' to get by this but resist the temptation.

Lastly, I've mentioned this in passing before but don't be the person who rings up their broker for investment advice. I mean, even Hollywood has figured out that this is a bad idea and has innumerable movies for you to learn from.

Your approach to trading determines how well you'll manage your risk. The real key to trading success is risk management and the simple math that underlines it.

CHAPTER 12: TECHNICAL ANALYSIS INDICATORS

Technical analysis is the method of using charts and other recording methods to analyze various data in options trading.

Using these visual instruments, you have the chance to determine the direction of the market because they give you a trend.

This method focuses on studying the supply and demand of a market. The price will be seen to rise when the investor realizes the market is undervalued, and this leads to buying. If they think that the market is overvalued, the prices will start falling, and this is deemed the perfect time to sell.

You need to understand the movement of the various indicators to make the perfect decision. This method works on the premise that history usually repeats itself – a huge change in the prices affects the investors in any situation.

History

Technical analysis has been used over the years in trades. The technical analysis methods have been used for over a hundred years to come up with deductions regarding the market.

In Asia, the use of technical analysis led to the development of candlestick techniques, and it forms the main charting techniques.

Over time, more tools and techniques have come up to help traders come up with predictions of the prices in various markets.

There are many indicators that you can use to determine the direction of the market, but only a few are valuable to your course. Let us look at the various indicators and how to use them.

Support and Resistance

These levels occur at points where both the buyer and the seller aren't dormant. These levels are displayed on the chart using a horizontal line extended in the past to the future.

The different prices reach at the support and resistance points in the future.

How to Apply Support and Resistance

• Using these points allows you to know when to call or put.

• Support and resistance give you a way to determine the entry point to

use for a directional trade.

The Significance of Trends in Option Trading

Technical analysis works on the premise of the trend. These trends come by due to the interaction of the buyer and the seller. The aggressiveness of one of the parties in the market will determine how steep the trend becomes. To make a profit, you have to take advantage of the changes in the price movement.

To understand the direction of the trend, you ought to look at the troughs and peaks and how they relate to each other.

When looking for money in options trading, you ought to trade with a trend. The trend is what determines the decision you make when faced with a situation – whether to buy or to sell. You need to know the various signs that a prevailing trend is soon ending so that you can manage the risks and exit the trades the right way.

Characteristics of Technical Analysis

This analysis makes use of models and trading rules using different price and volume changes. These include the volume, price, and other different market info.

Technical analysis is applied among financial professionals and traders and is used by many option traders.

The Principles of Technical analysis

Many traders on the market use the price to come up with information that affects the decision you make ultimately. The analysis looks at the trading pattern and what information it offers you rather than looking at drivers such as news events, economic and fundamental events.

Price action usually tends to change every time because the investor leans towards a certain pattern, which in turn predicts trends and conditions.

Prices Determine Trends

Technical analysts know that the price in the market determines the trend of the market. The trend can be up, down, or move sideways.

History Usually Repeats Itself

Analysts believe that an investor repeats the behavior of the people that traded before them. The investor sentiment usually repeats itself. Due to the fact that the behavior repeats itself, traders know that using a price pattern can lead to predictions.

The investor uses the research to determine if the trend will continue or if the reversal will stop eventually and will anticipate a change when the charts show a lot of investor sentiment.

Combination with Other Analysis Methods

To make the most out of the technical analysis, you need to combine it with other charting methods on the market. You also need to use secondary data, such as sentiment analysis and indicators.

To achieve this, you need to go beyond pure technical analysis, and combine other market forecast methods in line with technical work.

You can use technical analysis along with fundamental analysis to improve the performance of your portfolio.

You can also combine technical analysis with economics and quantitative analysis. For instance, you can use neural networks along with technical analysis to identify the relationships in the market. Other traders make use of technical analysis with astrology.

Other traders go for newspaper polls, sentiment indicators to come with deductions.

The Different Types of Charts Used in Technical Analysis Candlestick Chart

This is a charting method that came from the Japanese. The method fills the interval between opening and closing prices to show a relationship. These candles use color coding to show the closing points. You will come across black, red, white, blue, or green candles to represent the closing point at any time.

Open-high-low-close Chart (OHLC)

These are also referred to as bar charts, and they give you a connection between the maximum and minimum prices in a trading period. They usually feature a tick on the left side to show the open price and one on the right to show the closing price.

Overlays

These are usually used on the main price charts and come in different ways:

• Resistance – refers to a price level that acts as the maximum level above the usual price

• Support – the opposite of resistance, and it shows as the lowest value of the price

• Trend line – this is a line that connects two troughs or peaks.

• Channel – refers to two trend lines that are parallel to each other

• Moving average – a kind of dynamic trendline that looks at the average price in the market

• Bollinger bands – these are charts that show the rate of volatility in a market.

• Pivot point – this refers to the average of the high, low, and closing price averages for a certain stock or currency.

Price-based Indicators

These analyze the price values of the market. These include:

• Advance decline line – this is an indicator of the market breadth

• Average directional index – shows the strength of a trend in the market

• Commodity channel index – helps you to identify cyclical trends in the market

• Relative strength index – this is a chart that shows you the strength of the price

• Moving average convergence (MACD) – this shows the point where two trend line converge or diverge.

• Stochastic oscillator – this shows the close position that has happened within the recent trading range

• Momentum – this is a chart that tells you how fast the price changes
The Benefits of Technical Analysis in Options Trading

There are a variety of benefits that you enjoy when you use technical analysis in trading options. The benefits arise from the fact that traders are usually asking a lot of questions touching on the price of the market and entry points. While the forecast for prices is a huge task, the use of technical analysis makes it easier to handle.

The major advantages of technical analysis include Expert Trend Analysis

This is the biggest advantage of technical analysis in any market. With this method, you can predict the direction of the market at any time. You can determine whether the market will move up, down or sideways easily.

Entry and Exit Points

As a trader, you need to know when to place a trade and when to opt out. The entry point is all about knowing the right time to enter the trade for good returns. Exiting a trade is also vital because it allows you to reduce losses.

Leverage Early Signals

Every trader looks for ways to get early signals to assist them in making decisions. Technical analysis gives you signals to trigger a decision on your part. This is usually ideal when you suspect that a trend will reverse soon. Remember the time the trend reverses are when you need to make crucial decisions.

It Is Quick

In options trading, you need to go with techniques that give you fast results. Additionally, getting technical analysis data is cheaper than other techniques in fundamental analysis, with some companies offering free charting programs. If you are in the market to make use of short time intervals such as 1-minute, 5-minute, 30 minute or 1-hour charts, you can get this using technical analysis.

It Gives You A Lot of Information

Technical analysis gives you a lot of information that you can use to make trading decisions. You can easily build a position depending on the information you get then take or exit trades. You have access to information such as chart pattern, trends, support, resistance, market momentum, and other information.

The current price of an asset usually reflects every known information of an asset. While the market might be rife with rumors that the prices might surge or plummet, the current price represents the final point for all information. As the traders and investors change their bearing from one part to another, the changes in asset reflect the current value perception.

If all this turns out to be true, then the only info you require is a price chart that gives all the price reflections and predictions. There isn't any need for you to worry yourself with the reasons why the price is rising or falling when you can use a chart to determine everything.

With the right technical analysis information, you can make trading easier and faster because you make decisions based not on hearsay but facts. You don't have to spend your time reading and trying to make headway in financial news. All you need us to check what the chart tells you.

You Understand Trends

If the prices on the market were to gyrate randomly without any direction, you would find it hard to make money. While these trends run in all directions, the prices always move in trends. Directional bias allows you to leverage the benefits of making money. Technical analysis allows you to determine when a trend occurs and when it doesn't occur, or when it is in reversal.

Many of the profitable techniques that are used by the traders to make money follow trends. This means that you find the right trend and then look for opportunities that allow you to enter the market in the same direction as the trend. This helps you to capitalize on the price movement.

Trends run in various degrees. The degree of the trend determines how much money you make, whether in the short term or long-term trading. Technical analysis gives you all the tools that make it possible for you to do this.

History Always Repeats Itself

Technical analysis uses common patterns to give you the information to trade. However, you need to understand that history will not be exact when it repeats itself, though. The current analysis will be either bigger or smaller, depending on the existing market conditions. The only thing is that it won't be a replica of the prior pattern.

This pans out easily because most human psychology doesn't change so much, and you will see that the emotions have a hand in making sure that prices rise and fall. The emotions that traders exhibit create a lot of patterns that lead to changes in prices all the time. As a trader, you need to identify these patterns and then use them for trading. Use prior history to guide you and then the current price as a trigger of the trade.

Enjoy Proper Timing

Do you know that without proper timing you will not be able to make money at all? One of the major advantages of technical analysis is that you get the chance to time the trades. Using technical analysis, you get to wait, then place your money in other opportunities until it is the right time to place a trade.

Applicable Over a Wide Time Frame

When you learn technical analysis, you get to apply it to many areas in different markets, including options. All the trading in a market is based mostly on the patters that are as a result of human behavior. These patterns can then be mapped out on a chart to be used across the markets.

While there is some difference between analyzing different securities, you will be able to use technical analysis in most of the markets.

Additionally, you can use the analysis in any timeframe, which is applicable whether you use hourly, daily, or weekly charts. These markets are usually taken to be fractal, which essentially means that patterns that appear on a small scale will also be present on a large scale as well.

Technical Analysis Secrets to Become the Best Trader

To make use of technical analysis the right way, you need to follow time- testing approaches that have made the technique a gold mine for many traders. Let us look at the various tips that will take you from novice to pro in just a few days:

Use More than One Indicator

Numbers make trading easy, but it also applies to the way you apply your techniques. For one, you need to know that just because one technical indicator is better than using one, applying a second indicator is better than using just one. The use of more than one indicator is one of the best ways to confirm a trend. It also increases the odds of being right.

As a trader, you will never be 100 percent right at all times, and you might even find that the odds are stashed against you when everything is plain to see. However, don't demand too much from your indicators such that you end up with analysis paralysis.

To achieve this, make use of indicators that complement each other rather than the ones that clash against each other.

Go For Multiple Time Frames

Using the same buy signal every day allows you to have confidence that the indicator is giving you all you need to know to trade. However, make sure you look for a way to use multiple timeframes to confirm a trend. When you have a doubt, it is wise that you increase the timeframe from an hour to a day or from a daily chart to a weekly chart.

Understand that No Indicator Measures Everything

You need to know that indicators are supposed to show how strong a trend is, they won't tell you much more. So, you need to understand and focus on what the indicator is supposed to communicate instead of working with assumptions.

Go With the Trend

If you notice that an option is trading upward, then go ahead and buy it. Conversely when the trend stops trending, then it is time to sell it. If you aren't sure of what is going on in the market at that time, then don't make a move.

However, waiting might make you lose profitable trades as opposed to trading. You also miss out on opportunities to create more capital.

Have the Right Skills

It really takes superior analytical capabilities and real skill to be successful at trading, just like any other endeavor. Many people think that it is hard to make money with options trading, but with the right approach, you can make extraordinary profits.

You need to learn and understand the various skills so that you know what the market seeks from you and how to achieve your goals.

Trade with a Purpose

Many traders go into options trading with the main aim of having a hobby. Well, this way you won't be able to make any money at all. What you need to do is to trade for the money – strive to make profits unlike those who try to make money as a hobby.

Always Opt for High value

Well, no one tells you to trade any security that comes your way – it is purely a matter of choice. Try and go for high-value options so that you can trade them the right way. Make use of fundamental analysis to choose the best options to trade in.

Be Disciplined

When using technical analysis, you might find yourself in situations that require you to make a decision fast. To achieve success, you need to have strict risk management protocols. Don't base on your track record to come up with choices; instead, make sure you follow what the analysis tells you.

Don't Overlook Your Trading Plan

The trading plan is in place to guide you when things go awry. Coming up with the plan is easy, but many people find it hard to implement the plan the right way. The trading plan has various components – the signals and the take-profit/stop-loss rules. Once you get into the market, you need to control yourself because you have already taken a leap. Remember you cannot control the indicators once they start running – all you can do is to prevent yourself from messing up everything.

Come up with the trading rules when you are unemotional to try and mitigate the effects of making bad decisions.

Accept Losses

Many people trade with one thing in mind – losses aren't part of their plan. This is a huge mistake because you need to understand that every trade has two sides to it – a loss and a profit. Remember that the biggest mistake that leads to losses isn't anything to do with bad indicators rather using them the wrong way. Always have a stop-loss order when you trade to prevent loss of money.

Have a Target When You Trade

So, what do you plan to achieve today? Remember, trading is a way to grow your capital as opposed to saving. Options trading is a business that has probable outcomes that you get to estimate. When you make a profit, make sure you take some money from the table and then put it in a safe place.

CHAPTER 13: IN-DEPTH
KNOWLEDGE OF INDICATORS

When you are engaging in options trading, you don't have to become an expert on stock charts the way that a day trader of stocks needs to be. However, it is a good idea to get some familiarity with the tools of trading so that you can make reasonably sound estimates of where a stock price is moving, which will translate into more winning trades for the options trader.

Also, as an options trader, as we mentioned above, you don't necessarily need to dive deeply into this subject, and you also don't need to be sitting at your computer staring at graphs and charts all day long. Most options traders are simply going to go with the flow of where stock prices are moving, rather than trying to get into the weeds of every last detail.

One reason for this is that changes in share prices are magnified through options. A change of a few tens of cents or dollars is big for the options trader but less significant for a stock trader. Second, a day trader is looking to make their profits over the course of a few hours, so they have to sit there staring at their computer screens waiting for the exact moment to enter and exit a trade, and they can't risk holding the kinds of positions they take overnight. As an options trader, despite the reputation for risk and complexity that comes along with options, you aren't going to be trading with the same constraints.

That said, knowing something about the technical analysis can help you be a more successful options trader. It will help you spot changing trends in prices and recognize the right times to enter and exit trades. Of course, this is more art than science, and there is no exact right time to do anything in the stock market, you are just playing your odds. That said, having the knowledge to recognize likely shifts in pricing trends can help you make better trades.

These are mathematical tools that are built to help traders get more information out of pricing trends in the markets. The tools of technical analysis should be viewed as aids as well, and far too many people get fooled into thinking they are infallible, rather than recognizing them for what they are, which is to provide assistance, not absolute and "true" answers.

The best approach to be taken is to combine a few tools together. What most traders do is look for an indication in one of their main ways to track stock market price changes, and then they will use another tool to either confirm or deny what they saw in the first place. Only when two or three different tools or indicators confirm the same pricing trend, do they take action in the markets.

As an options trader – you are going to be applying these tools to the pricing of the underlying stock and not to the option itself. So, if you are interested in trading options on Facebook, you are going to be studying the trading behavior of the Facebook stock, and not the options. When you see favorable changes in the Facebook stock, then you will go ahead and make moves with your options trades.

Candlestick Charts

A candlestick chart is a method of plotting financial data that tells you how prices moved over a given trading session. Rather than having a continuous curve, the price data is broken down into different time frames. There is not a specific time frame that is used; you can create candlestick charts using various time frames. For example, you can have a chart break up a trading day into fifteen-minute increments. Then, the candlesticks will be created for each fifteen-minute increment throughout each trading day, and it will give you pricing information for each of those increments. You can break prices down by the minute, by five-minutes, by an hour, by four hours, and so on.

Candlestick charts are quite general in their application. They can be used for any financial asset that is traded in real-time. In fact, they were originally developed in Japan, to track changes in the price of rice. So, they can be used for commodities, stocks, bonds, Forex, or any other asset. Naturally, they are used for stocks, which is why we are discussing them, and our discussion will be focused on that.

Looking at the basic unit of a candlestick chart, which is a trading session of the selected time length, the first thing to look at is the color. At a glance, the color of a candlestick tells you the direction of price movement in that trading session. There are different color schemes used on charts, but for stocks, it is typical to use a white background. If the price of the stock went up over the time period, then the color is going to be green. If the price of the stock dropped over the time period, the color is going to be red.

The candlestick is going to have a "body" and "wicks" coming out of it (in some treatments, the wicks are referred to as "shadows"). The length of the body tells you how much the price moved over the course of the entire trading session. This information is to be taken in conjunction with the color of the candlestick.

If the candlestick is green, then the bottom of the candlestick is the opening price for the trading session (low in value), and the top of the candlestick is the closing price of the trading session (high in value – so the price rose over the trading session).

If the candlestick is red, the relationships are reversed. In this case, the top of the candlestick is the opening price for the trading session. Then, the bottom of the candlestick is going to be the lower, closing price of the trading session, reflecting that the stock lost value over the time period.

Red and green candlesticks are also referred to by the mood they represent. If a candlestick is red, the mood is "bearish" since people are getting out of the stock, and so it can be referred to as a bearish candlestick. Conversely, if the mood is bullish, prices are rising, and people are trying to buy into the stock, and so, a green candlestick is bullish.

The wicks on a candlestick have the same meaning regardless of color. The top wick is the high price attained during the trading session, and the bottom wick is the low price seen during the trading session.

Candlesticks can help you determine the momentum of trading. If the wicks are long, but the body is short, that helps you determine that there was a large push of the price in one direction or another, but there was not enough momentum to sustain it, and prices ended up moving back to where they were when the trading session opened, or at least relatively close by.

Remember that pricing is related to supply and demand. So, if prices are rising, there is more demand for the stock. If prices are dropping, people are dumping the stock (increasing the supply), and demand is decreasing.

Candlesticks and Trends

The main way that candlesticks are used is to spot changes in price trends. So, you want to be paying close attention to candlesticks when the stock price has been dropping or rising for a period of time, and you are looking for signals that a reversal in the price trend is about to occur.

A sudden shift from selling to buying or vice versa is one way that a trend reversal can be noted. This is indicated by an "enveloping" candlestick. That is, you have a candlestick of one type that is larger than the preceding candlestick of the opposite type, then you have a situation where a trend reversal is indicated.

Take, for example, the situation where stock prices have been declining. You are going to see some fluctuation, but there is going to be largely a trend of red candlesticks reflecting the trend of dropping prices. When you see a small red candlestick followed by a bullish candlestick that has a body that is large enough to completely engulf the body of the bearish or red candlestick that preceded it, this is usually a sign that the sell-off is over, and prices are going to start rising. So, this is an indication that you want to buy a call option (or sell a put option) on the stock at this point. When prices are rising, you look for a bearish candlestick to engulf a bullish candlestick to indicate that peak price has been reached, and people are going to start selling off the stock.

Another indicator of a change in trend is when you have seen a trend in one direction, and then you see three candlesticks in a row of the opposite type. Let's consider a downward trend in prices first. If prices have been dropping, then you see three green or bullish candlesticks in a row, particularly when each succeeding candlestick has a higher closing price, this is a solid indication that prices are going to reverse, and the stock is entering an upward price trend. On the other hand, if you are at the top of an uptrend, and you see three bearish candlesticks in a row, each with lower closing prices than the preceding candlestick, that tells you that the stock price is probably going to start dropping.

Of course, these are rules of thumb; they are not exact or guaranteed to lead to the results described. They often or usually do, but you should confirm these signals using another tool before making major trading decisions.

Moving Averages

There are many more signals that you can get from candlestick charts, but the most potent technical indicator that can be used to detect price trend reversals is the moving average. However, a lot of the price movements are nothing more than noise. It would be nice to smooth out the data to eliminate that noise so that we could get a smooth curve that represents the actual underlying price movement of the asset. This can be done, and it is done by averaging the prices of the stock over a given time period.

By taking the average of a given number of past time periods together, and calculating it at each point along the line, we can generate what is called a moving average. You can have a simple moving average, which just gives you the straightforward arithmetic average of the prices used. Or you can use other moving averages that weight prices, giving more weight to recent prices as opposed to earlier prices. The most popular weighted moving average is the exponential moving average.

The Relative Strength Indicator

Now, let's turn our attention to the relative strength indicator, which is a curve that you can add below your stock chart. This is also known as the RSI.

The purpose of the RSI is to give you an idea of whether a financial asset is overbought or oversold. Whenever there is a financial asset being traded, the asset has some real value that represents what it is worth in terms of fundamentals. However, people get frantic buying up assets, and this can drive asset prices to a higher level than they are actually worth. You can think of the 2008 financial crisis as a good, if not an extreme example. During that time, housing prices had been bid far above what actual market conditions justified.

In most cases, stock prices are not going to be bid up high to that extent, but the phenomenon of buyers coming in and bidding up prices to artificially high levels that are not financially justifiable is something that always happens. When you are studying changing stock prices looking for the right time to get in or out of your trades, it is hard to guess accurately when this point has been reached. While it is not perfect and not an absolute, the RSI does give you a helpful tool you can use to estimate when stocks have been overbought or oversold.

If the RSI has a value between 70-100, this means that the asset is overbought. When an asset is overbought, the price can continue rising for a little while, but at some point, the steam is going to run out on the price increases, and people are going to start selling off the stock because they don't want to lose their profits. When the sell off becomes crown behavior, that means that options prices are going to start dropping. So when the RSI enters this range, you might take it to mean that you should sell call options and buy put options. You can confirm what the RSI is telling you by looking at the values of the moving averages and your candlestick charts.

Bollinger Bands

The final big indicator that is useful for options traders to at least take a look at is a tool called the Bollinger bands. Bollinger bands contain of three curves – a top, midline, and bottom curve. The midline curve is a simple moving average of stock prices. The curve at the top is one or two standard deviations above the moving average. Typically, two standard deviations are used, but it is your decision. Finally, the bottom curve is one or two standard deviations below the moving average.

This is plotted on top of a candlestick chart. What you are going to look for here is that the candlesticks either stay in between the curves representing the boundaries of the standard deviations from the mean or if they touch them or go outside. If the stock price has been rising, and you see candlesticks going outside the upper band, this is an indication that the stock price has been pushed up too far, and a price reversal is likely. So, in that case, if you are invested in call options, you might want to sell them off. Or, it could indicate a good time to buy put options since prices are probably going to start dropping.

On the other hand, consider declining stock prices. If they touch or go outside the lower Bollinger band, that is an indication that prices are probably going to reverse, and you are probably going to see an upward trend in prices. So, it indicates that is a good time to buy call options and to sell put options. They are certainly a very useful indicator, but you probably don't want to engage in trading based solely on what the Bollinger bands are telling you. Instead, you are going to want to combine multiple indicators together to make your decisions. The larger a trade is, the more seriously you are going to want to take this.

Which Indicators to Use

The choice of tools to use in determining when to enter and exit your trades is a matter of personal taste. Most or virtually all traders use candlestick charts, but it is important to keep in mind that options traders don't need to be paying as much attention to the nitty-gritty details as a day stock trader or swing trader does.

Moving averages are one tool that will prove to be extremely useful for any trader. If you only use moving averages together with candlestick charts, you probably have your bases covered when it comes to determining how to manage your trades of call and put options. Going beyond this with the RSI or Bollinger bands can help solidify your trading decisions, but whether or not that is necessary is debatable, and you should just do what you feel makes you confident in trading. There are also many additional technical indicators that are used by stock traders that you may find useful.

CHAPTER 14: COMMON MISTAKES AMONG BEGINNERS

I get hundreds of emails every day from traders and investors. If you can avoid these mistakes when you are just getting started, you will be way ahead of the pack and will also save yourself a lot of losses and misery. Write down these "5 Commandments" on a sticky note and put it on your computer screen:

1.Don't buy stocks that are hitting 52-week lows.

2.Don't trade penny stocks.

3.Don't short stocks.

4.Don't trade on margin.

5.Don't trade other people's ideas.

1.Don't buy stocks that are hitting 52-week lows.

So many new traders lose a lot of money trying to catch the proverbial "falling knife." In spite of what everyone will tell you, you are almost always much better off buying a stock that is hitting 52-week highs than one hitting 52-week lows.

Has a company that you own just reported some really bad news? If so, remember that there is never just one cockroach. Bad news comes in clusters. Many investors recently learned this the hard way with General Electric, which just kept reporting one bad thing after another, causing the stock to crash from 30 to 7. There is no such thing as a "safe stock." Even a blue chip stock can go down a lot if it loses its competitive advantage or the company makes bad decisions.

A cascade of bad news can often cause a stock to trend down or gap down repeatedly. If you own a stock that does this, it is often better to get out and wait a few months (or years) to reenter. Again, there is never just one cockroach.

Never buy a stock after you have seen the first cockroach. When a stock goes down a lot, it can affect the company's fundamentals as well. Employee and management morale will deteriorate, the best employees may leave the company, and it may become more difficult for the company to raise money by selling shares or issuing debt.

Conversely, when a stock goes up a lot, it can improve the company's fundamentals. Employee and management morale will be high, everyone at the company will want to work harder, it will be easier to recruit new talent, and it will become easier for the company to raise money by issuing stock or debt.

If you stick to stocks that are trading above their 200-day moving averages, or that are hitting 52-week highs, you will do much better than trying to catch falling knives.

2.Don't trade penny stocks.

A penny stock is any stock that trades under $5. Unless you are an advanced trader, you should avoid all penny stocks. I would extend this by encouraging you to also avoid all stocks priced under $10.

Even if you have a small trading account ($5,000) or less, you are better off buying fewer shares of a higher-priced stock than a lot of shares of a penny stock.

That is because low-priced stocks are most often associated with lower quality companies. As a result, they are not usually allowed to trade on the NYSE or the Nasdaq. Instead, they trade on the OTCBB ("over the counter bulletin board") or Pink Sheets, both of which have much less stringent financial reporting requirements than the major exchanges do.

Many of these companies have never made a profit. They may be frauds or shell companies that are designed solely to enrich management and other insiders. They may also include former "blue chips" that have fallen on hard times like Eastman Kodak or Lehman Brothers.

In addition, penny stocks are inherently more volatile than higher-priced stocks. Think of it this way: if a $100 stock moves $1, that is a 1% move. If a $5 stock moves $1, that is a 20% move. Many new traders underestimate the kind of emotional and financial damage that this kind of volatility can cause.

In my experience, penny stocks do not trend nearly as well as higher-priced stocks. They tend to be more mean-reverting (Mean reversion occurs when a stock moves up sharply from its average trading price, only to fall right back down again to its average trading price). Many of them are eventually headed to zero, but they are still not good short candidates. Most brokers will not let you short them. And even if you do find a broker who will let you short a penny stock, how would you like to wake up to see your penny stock trading at $10 when you just shorted it at $2 a few days before? I learned that lesson the hard way. It turned out that I was risking $8 to make $2, which is not a good way to make money over the long term.

To add injury to insult, a penny stock might appear to be liquid one day, and the next day, the liquidity dries up and you are confronted by a $2 bid/ask spread. Or the bid might completely disappear. Imagine owning a stock for which there are now no buyers.

Stay away from all stocks under $10. Also stay away from trading newsletters that hawk penny stocks. The owners of these newsletters are often paid by the companies themselves to hype their stocks. Or they may take a position in a penny stock, send out an email telling everyone to buy it, and then sell their stock at a much higher price to these amateur buyers.

Watch the movie "The Wolf of Wall Street" if you'd like to see a famous example of the decadent lifestyle and fraud that often surround penny stocks. Viewer discretion is advised.

Don't short stocks.

In order to short a stock, you must first borrow shares of the stock from your broker. You then sell those shares on the open market. If the stock falls in price, you will be able to buy back those shares at a lower price for a profit. If, however, the stock goes up a lot, you may be forced to buy back the shares at a much higher price, and end up losing more money than you ever had in your trading account to begin with.

In November 2015, Joe Campbell broke 2 of the 5 commandments. He first decided to trade a penny stock called KaloBios Pharmaceuticals. To make things worse, he decided to short it.

When he went to bed that evening, his trading account was worth roughly $37,000. When he woke up the next morning, the stock had skyrocketed. As a result, not only had he lost all of the $37,000, but he now owed his broker an additional $106,000.

And there was no way out. If you owe your broker money, they can haul you into court and go after your house and savings.

Sometimes even the wealthiest investors can be wiped out by shorting a stock. During the great Northern Pacific Corner of 1901, shares of that railroad stock went from $170 to $1,000 in a single day. That move bankrupted some of the wealthiest Americans of the day, who had shorted the stock and were then forced to cover at higher prices.

If you do end up shorting a stock, remember that your broker will charge you a fee (usually expressed as an annual interest rate) to borrow the stock. In addition, if you are short a stock, you are responsible for paying any dividends on that stock (your broker will automatically take the money out of your account quarterly).

For all of these reasons, shorting stocks is clearly an advanced and risky trading strategy. Don't try it until you've been trading for at least 5 years, and you have the financial stability to withstand a freakish upwards move in a stock.

And never short a penny stock. It's just not worth it.

3.Don't trade on margin.

In order to short a stock, you will need to open up a margin account with your broker, as Joe Campbell did. You'll also need a margin account in order to trade stocks using margin.

When you buy a stock on margin, it means that you are borrowing money from your broker, in order to purchase more shares of stock than you would normally be able to buy with just the cash sitting in your brokerage account.

Let's say that I have $10,000 in my margin account. Most brokers in the U.S. will allow me to go on margin to purchase $20,000 worth of stock in that account. What this means is that they are lending me an additional $10,000 (usually at some outrageous annual interest rate like 11%, which is what E*Trade currently charges) to buy more shares of stock.

If I buy $10,000 worth of stock and the stock goes up 10%, I've just made $1,000. But if I can increase the amount of stock that I'm buying to $20,000 using a margin loan, I will have made $2,000 on the same 10% move. That will mean that my trading account has just gone up by 20% ($2,000/$10,000).

Of course, if the stock goes down 10% and I'm on full margin, I will have lost 20% of my account value. Trading on margin is thus a form of leverage: it amplifies the performance of your portfolio both on the upside and the downside.

When you buy a stock using margin, the stock and cash in your trading account is held as collateral for the margin loan. If the stock falls enough, you may be required to add more cash to your account immediately (this is called "getting a margin call"), or risk having the broker force you to immediately sell your stock to raise cash. Often this will lead to your selling the stock at the worst possible time.

When you open up a new brokerage account and you are given the choice of a "cash account" or a "margin account," it's OK to pick "margin account." A margin account has certain advantages, such as being able to use the proceeds from selling a stock to immediately buy another stock without having to wait a few days for the trade to settle. If you never exceed your cash buying power in a margin account, you will never be charged fees or interest. In that way, it's quite possible to have a margin account, but never to go on margin.

If, however, you don't trust yourself, open up a "cash account." That

way, you will never be allowed to trade on margin.

4.Don't trade other people's ideas.

There are two main reason for this.

The first reason never to trade someone else's ideas is that they probably don't know what they are doing. If you get a hot stock tip from your neighbor or at the gym, it's best to ignore it. They probably have no idea what they are talking about.

Second, even if you get a really good and legitimate trading or investing idea from someone else, you will probably not have the conviction to hold on to it when the going gets tough. That conviction can only come from developing a trade idea yourself. When you have designed a trade, or researched an investment for yourself, you will have the conviction to hold on. You will also know where your stop loss is, in case the stock goes south. Have you noticed how hot stock tips never come with a recommended stop loss level?

Also, never place a trade based on something that you have just read in Barron's, Forbes, The Wall Street Journal, or have just seen on CNBC. Never buy a stock based on an analyst upgrade, or sell a stock based on an analyst downgrade.

I've seen analysts finally downgrade a stock only once it has fallen 50%.

Analysts are lagging indicators. They tend to upgrade stocks that have already moved up, and downgrade stocks that have already moved down. There is also a strong selection bias among analysts. The best analysts get hired by hedge funds, and you never hear from them again. The worst analysts stay at the banks or brokerage houses, and continue to dispense their mediocre advice. Huge amounts of money have been lost by following their advice.

Should you even follow Warren Buffett's advice? Yes, and no. His advice is definitely much better than a hot stock tip from your neighbor. On the other hand, if you listened to him religiously, you missed out on all of the great tech stocks of the last 20 years. He waited until Apple and Amazon were up many thousands of percentage points before finally purchasing them.

Anyone can learn to think for themselves in the stock market, and come up with their own trading and investing ideas.

Rather than giving you a fish, I would much rather teach you how to fish for yourself. That is the path to true financial freedom.

CHAPTER 15: MONEY MANAGEMENT

Should you hire a professional financial adviser to help you in the management of your portfolio and your investment?

First off, it's important to mention that many people now realize that they cannot solely depend on a financial advisor to manage their portfolios. The crashing of stocks and other markets in recent years has established the need for anyone who is investing in any market to do some form of research and ensure that they gain knowledge in that area. In other words, whether you end up hiring a financial adviser or not, you cannot afford to slack off in learning about the stock market, as well as doing research on any stock that you buy. After all, it makes no sense to trust someone else with your money when you have no idea what they are planning to do with it.

Choosing or Using a Financial Advisor

A financial advisor is someone that helps you manage your money. They help you manage how you invest, save, and spend money. A financial advisor usually offers a wide range of services on everything that has to do with money. Now, the level of influence and interaction that the financial advisor has with your funds is up to you and the structure between both parties, that is, you and the advisor. The term financial advisor covers a wide range of services, ranging from investment planning, financial consulting and certified financial planners. There are also digital financial management options such as robo-advisors, where you are not necessarily interacting with a human manager.

What can a Financial Advisor do for you?

A financial advisor is an expert in financial matters, who provides various services hinged upon managing money, investments, and savings. Therein lies the core of financial advising. The influence of technology has made it possible for ordinary people to enter into the financial market without going through the formal training necessarily. That said, certain kinds of knowledge are available to only those who are formally trained financially and can access and take advantage of. In other words, the fact that you can access the stock market, in some form at least, and make trades does not mean that you know everything that there is to know about the market. This is where a financial advisor comes in.

A financial advisor can, among many other things, help you assess your financial situation, set or evaluate your financial goals, and help you chart a path to achieve those goals. So, a financial advisor will examine your assets, expenses, and debts, and then help you identify how exactly you can improve. They can also help you work to reduce spending, figure out insurance and tax, increase your savings, and invest your money. Since a financial advisor has professional expertise and experience, they can help you improve your portfolio significantly. A good financial advisor can be of help when it comes to achieving your goals of financial independence and freedom.

Types of Financial Advisors

There are quite several types of financial advisors, both in terms of services offered and the contexts in which the services are provided.

Let's take a look at some of these financial advisors:

CFP: A CFP or Certified Financial Planner helps you do just that, plan your finances. A CFP must be licensed by a professional board in your country, such as the Certified Financial Planning Board of Standards in the U.S. To become a CFP, they must be educated thoroughly, pass through a rigorous test and demonstrate some level of work experience. These kinds of financial advisors are primarily aimed at helping you create goals, actionable goals for your finances that you should follow to achieve your goal as you go on.

Broker/Stockbroker: This kind of financial advisor assists you with investments and explains how to invest your money. A stockbroker buys or sells financial products (i.e., stocks) for their customers and typically receives a fee for doing this. To become a broker, you must be licensed by the U.S Security and Exchanges Commission in the US or any other equivalent board in any country where you may be based.

A Registered Investment Advisor: This kind of advisor gives advice and recommendations to investors for certain. RIAs are usually registered with the Security and Exchange Commission, or some other form of investor, depending on how large or small the company is. Some of these Investment advisors tend to focus on investment port-folios, while others seem to take on a more general and holistic view.

Also, it is not uncommon for a particular individual or company to offer the services of more than just one specific discipline. The reason for this is that it is not very realistic for an average person to employ a CFP only to plan their finances, and simultaneously employ another broker to manage financial instruments and other investments solely. Many individual financial advisors are licensed to act in multiple offices, or the company that they work for offers these services as part of a particular package.

How much does it cost to hire a Financial Advisor?

Perhaps you are already thinking; if a financial advisor is this good, or can offer this level of services, then I should probably patronize them;

well, pump your brakes first. You need to consider the cost implications of hiring a financial advisor. Many advisors charge different types of fees and at different rates, but here are some of the more common ones.

Hourly Rates: Some advisors charge between £75 per hour to about £350 per hour. In the UK, for example, the rates tend to hover around £150.

Set Fees: Some Financial advisors also request a fixed fee for performing a specific piece of work. It could range from a couple hundred to even a thousand dollars.

Monthly Fees: This option is usually reserved for those who are planning to use the advisor or their company's services for a long time. The advisor and the client can work out a specific fee that will be paid monthly for as long as you utilize their services. The fee could also be a portion of the money that you were seeking to invest.

Manage an Ongoing Fee: This scenario is closely related to that of paying a monthly fee for a service that is ongoing.

These are some of the combinations of fees that can be charged by financial advisors, and as you can see, they are quite expensive. Imagine that you have to pay a monthly service fee or a percentage of your investment money for the rest of your life, and it becomes costly. It is for this reason that many people are skeptical about using a Financial Advisor.

Should You Use a Financial Advisor?

The choice of whether to use a financial advisor, in the form of a broker, a CFP, or an Investment Advisor, is more of a personal one, rather than a general one. In other words, you have to look at your personal circumstances and see if it fits with your budget, time, and personal investment strategy.

One of the things that you need to consider is the kind of investments that you are making and how risky they are. Generally, the more risk you are willing to take on, the more you should be willing to use the services of a financial advisor. For example, if you are investing in mutual funds, there is little, if any, need for a financial advisor. However, if you are looking to enter the stock market to purchase individual stocks, then the risks you are taking on are more significant, and you might want to employ the services of a professional to assist you in managing the portfolio.

Another point to consider is the size of your portfolio. The larger your portfolio is, the more likely it is that you will need professional advice. Plus, a broader portfolio account can easily absorb the fees associated with hiring a financial advisor.

Finally, you should take out time to do your research before using a financial advisor. One of the best ways to get a financial advisor is to ask people around you who have enjoyed success in the stock market over a consistent period. While past profits are not a guarantee of future earnings, it is easier to trust someone that has a record of being somewhat successful than someone who hasn't had much success in the market.

If possible, try to create a list of as many advisors that you'd like to speak to, and schedule a conversation with them. You should do that offline, by the way. While online interviews and conversations are good starters, you should not decide to trust a person or company with your hard- earned money without at least meeting them. When you meet, ask questions about their investment strategy, whose trading style and philosophy they subscribe to, and how they plan to manage your portfolio. Most of the time, the first consultation is free, as it allows you to get to know each other without the pressure of finances forcing you to perform. The other thing is, as this is free, you have the choice to meet several and choose one whose mentality suits yours.

When you meet, ensure that you do not leave the meeting with any doubts about what you're getting into. Do not allow yourself to be bamboozled with high-sounding and complex language that you do not understand. I mean, you must insist that every term that you do not understand is explained, and every service charge is explained. Of course, you must be fair in your dealings too. Your advisor is a professional and deserves to be paid well for their expertise and sometimes experience.

Digital Alternatives to Financial Advisors

In recent times, more brokerage companies have been implementing digital investment management solutions. Two of these new developments are robo-advisors and Online Financial Planning services.

A robo-advisor is a digital service that offers simplified and low-cost investment management. To make use of it, you answer a few questions on the brokerage company's website, and then complex algorithms help you build an investment portfolio according to the goals that you have set and the risk appetite that you have indicated that you are comfortable with. In this way, robo-advisors help monitor and balance your investment, ensuring that your portfolio is managed correctly. What's more, a robo-advisor costs a fraction of what a real-life human financial advisor will cost.

Another option is online financial planning services. This is much closer to traditional advisors than a robo-advisor. The online service gives you access to human financial advisors who can help you manage your investments, among other things. Some packages grant access to the type of automated investments that you'll get from a robo-advisor, as well as the ability to consult with a team of financial advisors. Some more expensive alternatives grant you access to the kind of one-on-one service that you will have received from a traditional offline advisor.

Surprisingly, both of these options are relatively cheap, as well as being flexible. Some companies even charge a large percentage of their fees from the profits that they help you make. Before you select a financial advisor, especially online, ensure that you understand everything that they are offering, possibly speak to their support teams to gain an understanding of what exactly you will be charged.

Mutual Funds

A mutual fund is a financial vehicle that is made up of a pool of money that has been collected from many investors. A professional money manager manages the portfolio of a mutual fund. They collate the assets of the funds and invest it in a diversified portfolio to produce gains for the investors. The objective of a mutual fund is to generate income for the investors, and as such, the portfolio is structured and maintained to match the goals of the investment, as stated in the mutual funds' prospectus.

Investing in a mutual fund gives individual investors such as yourself access to a professionally managed and diversified portfolio of bonds, equities, stocks, and other securities. Every shareholder will gain and lose proportionally to the gain and losses that the funds make. Mutual funds tend to invest in a large number of securities, and the overall performance of the fund is tracked as a change in the market capitalization of the fund, which is an aggregated performance of the individual investments in the portfolio.

Understanding Mutual Funds in Depth

A mutual fund works by aggregating money from multiple investors to build an extensive portfolio, and then invest that money in various types of assets. These include bonds, securities, and equities. Thus, the overall value of the mutual fund depends on how each security or assets that are bought perform. So, in purchasing a unit of a mutual fund, you are buying into the mutual funds' performance or, better still, a part of the portfolio's value. You have invested your money into buying a fraction of many types of assets - a condition that you could not have carried were you to invest on your own. This is what makes a mutual fund different from other types of stock investments. The fact that a share in a mutual fund represents a share in many different stocks and other assets.

It is for this reason that the price of a share of a mutual fund is called the Net Asset Value (NAV) per share, or sometimes referred to as the NAPS. A mutual fund's NAV is found by dividing the total value of all the securities it holds by the total number of outstanding shares. Outstanding shares are the shares held by all institutional investors, shareholders, insiders, and company officers. Also, the value of a mutual fund's share can be bought or redeemed at the current NAV, which remains stable, unlike the price of a stock. The NAV of a mutual fund does not fluctuate but is settled at the end of each trading day.

Income is earned from a mutual fund in 3 major ways:

• Interest is earned on the dividends in stocks and interests on bonds held in the portfolio of the funds. Generally, a fund pays out a majority of the funds that it receives in a single year to investors in the form of a distribution. Usually, there is an option for investors to either receive a check or reinvest the earnings to get more shares.

• If the fund sells assets that have appreciated, then the fund is said to have a capital gain. Most funds also transfer these gains to the investors during a distribution at the end of a financial year.

Should you invest in a mutual fund?

Why should you consider investing in a mutual fund? Well, for starters, mutual funds help eliminate or at least reduce risk. Diversification is essential to keep your risks low. Or put in simple language, you shouldn't put all your eggs in one basket. Consider an investor that invests in Apple or Amazon stocks. Now, if the buy came just before the company had a lousy quarter, then the investor would lose a great deal of money because all his investment is tied to that particular company.

On the other hand, if the investor had used that money to buy shares in a mutual fund, then the loss will be mitigated. That is because the mutual fund has stocks in other companies; the loss will count for a little part of the fund's portfolio. In this way, a mutual fund helps you avoid any significant losses, but at the same time, you don't get any big wins either.

Imagine the flip-side of our analogy, where Amazon or Apple had a great quarter and outperformed the competition. Any investor that invested solely in that company would have made a lot of money. On the other hand, an investor in a mutual fund with a stake in a company will not make as much profit, because that company's stocks are only a part of the fund's portfolio. It's a classic risk and reward scenario: the higher your risk, the higher your chances of reward and vice versa.

It is important to say that if you are already investing in a retirement package, then you are most likely investing in some sort of mutual fund. In this case, you can decide to go for a riskier alternative. You might decide to invest directly in the stocks of a company.

While you can invest in the stock market on your own, sometimes, it may make sense to look at hiring the services of a professional financial advisor. However, the fees charged by many traditional professional advisors are quite high and can hurt your portfolio, especially if it isn't large. A good alternative is a robo-advisor or an online financial planning system. These digital platforms provide financial services similar to a traditional financial advisor but usually at a much cheaper rate. They take into consideration your present financial situation as well as your goals and help you plan how to achieve them. Lastly, you can invest in a mutual fund if you are seeking a way to diversify your investment and reduce risk. However, you should know that your profit might tend to be on the low end. Remember, once again, high risk, high reward, and low risk, low reward.

CONCLUSIONS

The next step is to step up your dedication to options trading! It's safe to say that if you already trading, there are probably things that you could be doing to take your options trading to the next level. The next step is to get into it. Even if this means that you're still not quite ready to begin options trading, you can still start to do more than simply read a book. For example, maybe this means that you set up meetings with a few brokers and compare commission costs, or maybe it means that you find a way to start trading in real-time via an application of some sort. The exact degree in which you want to pursue the options trading path is up to you, as long as you take the next steps towards making serious money!

www.ingramcontent.com/pod-product-compliance
Lightning Source LLC
Chambersburg PA
CBHW071708210326
41597CB00017B/2388